MA

# The Day I Fired Alan Ladd and Other World War II Adventures

## Also by A. E. Hotchner

The Dangerous American
Papa Hemingway
Treasure
King of the Hill
Looking for Miracles
Doris Day
Sophia: Living and Loving
The Man Who Lived at the Ritz
Choice People
Hemingway and His World
Blown Away
Louisiana Purchase
After the Storm

*Plays*

Sweet Prince
The Hemingway Hero
The Short Happy Life
The White House
Café Universe
Welcome to the Club
Exactly Like You
The World of Nick Adams

# The Day I Fired Alan Ladd and Other World War II Adventures

## A. E. Hotchner

University of Missouri Press
Columbia and London

Library of Congress Cataloging-in-Publication Data

Hotchner, A. E.
  The Day I Fired Alan Ladd and Other World War II
Adventures / A. E. Hotchner.
    p.  cm.
  ISBN 0-8262-1432-0 (acid-free paper)
  1. United States, Army Air Forces—Biography. 2. World War,
1939–1945—Personal narratives, American. I. Hotchner, A. E.
D811.H723 A3 2002

                    2002072778

Designer: Jennifer Cropp
Typesetter: Bookcomp, Inc.
Printer and binder: The Maple-Vail Book Manufacturing Group
Typefaces: Minion and Peignot

The author extends his appreciation to David Carkeet and
*Natural Bridge* for having published an excerpt of this book.

For Virginia, Ginny, and Ginger

# Preface

What I discovered about war is that despite one's best effort, it is not easy to be heroic. I'm talking about a live hero. Dead is not as difficult. To perform heroically in a perilous situation is one thing, but I found that, in my case, the real difficulty was in getting myself into a spot where heroism was possible. Nobody on latrine duty ever got the Medal of Honor.

For four years I twisted and turned through the labyrinth of the military establishment without ever arriving at the zenith of my search, which was to find a way to engage the enemy and through deed and daring conquer him heroically. I know that sounds naive but I assure you that in 1942, with nineteen ships of our Pearl Harbor fleet in smoldering ruins and twenty-four hundred of our people dead plus the fact that Hitler was ravaging Europe, the desire for patriotic retribution was real. But the more I tried to perform what I perceived was my duty, the more the unpredictable finger of military fate kept pointing me in the opposite direction. The way I see it, heroism in the military is divided into three categories: men who try to be heroic and fail; men who try and succeed; and men who never get a chance, of which I am a prime example, as you will see in this account of my four-year career in the Air Force. I rose through the ranks from private to major, hoping with each promotion to be put in harm's way, but harm avoided me, not me it.

The best laid schemes o' mice an' men
Gang aft agley.

Robert Burns

# The Day I Fired Alan Ladd and Other World War II Adventures

# ONE

On Wednesday, October 16, 1940, I stood on line for six hours in the basement of the Heman Grammar School in St. Louis, Missouri, in order to get a number thrust upon me by the United States government. It was to be my identification in a military bingo game that had been devised by Franklin Delano Roosevelt, the president of the United States.

Sixteen million other young men were also on line that day in towns and cities across the country, all of us involuntarily summoned by announcements such as this one, which had run on the front page of the *St. Louis Post-Dispatch*:

### REGISTRATION
If you are a man who has reached his 21st birthday but has not reached his 36th birthday, you must register today for selective service.

If you have no valid reason for failing to do so you are liable to arrest, and if convicted you may be sentenced to as much as five years in prison and fined $10,000.

You are to register between 7 A.M. and 9 P.M. at the nearest school in the election district in which you live or where you are staying if you are from out of town. If you have used your best efforts to locate your registration place and cannot find it, inquire at the police station nearest where you are staying.

Despite the somber tone of this summons, the atmosphere in the Heman School basement that morning was actually quite jolly. The gathering was in effect a giant neighborhood reunion as we all wandered up and down greeting old friends we hadn't seen for years. Shouts of recognition and laughter filled the air and no one there seemed to feel that this numbering procedure was cause for concern. Certainly I didn't.

Although the world seethed with military activity, our country was not at war with anyone, life was good (as compared with the dreadful years of the Depression, which was just tapering off), and President Roosevelt himself had assured us, "I have said this before, but I shall say it again and again and again: Your boys are not going to be sent into any foreign wars." So despite the fact that the Nazis had already conquered Austria, Czechoslovakia, Poland, Denmark, Norway, the Netherlands, and Belgium, and that only a few months before, the Wehrmacht had overrun the vaunted Maginot Line and brought France to its knees with only the heroics of the Dunkirk evacuation saving the 350,000 British and French soldiers who had been trapped on the Channel coast—despite these grim military events in Europe and the equally grim military activity by the Japanese forces in the Pacific, my friends and I felt assured that we would never be drawn into any of it.

The Midwest was entrenched in isolationism and the voice that carried the most weight with us belonged to our very own St. Louis hero, Colonel Charles A. Lindbergh. My own hero worship of Lindy went far back to February 14, 1928, when, as a second grader, I had gone to the Mississippi levee along with all the rest of the St. Louis schoolchildren and watched with openmouthed adoration and wonderment as Lindbergh flew a special mission for us schoolkids in his *Spirit of St. Louis,* the very plane that he had recently flown across the Atlantic. We had been transported to the levee in a fleet of gaily decorated streetcars, our names carefully tagged onto our coats. After an hour's wait we were rewarded with the appearance, on the far side of the Eads Bridge, of the white speck that quickly magnified into the *Spirit of St. Louis.*

Lindy flew low over our heads and waggled his wings and waved to us through the open window of his cockpit. We cheered with all our might and called his name again and again in a high-pitched chorus as he circled and circled above us, the name *Spirit of St. Louis* easy to read on the little plane's white nose. Then Lindbergh suddenly wheeled away from us and we groaned disappointment at his departure, but no! He was not leaving but only preparing to give us one of the great thrills of our young lives. He followed the Mississippi River beyond the Eads Bridge, then abruptly nosed the plane around in a full circle and headed back toward us as we screamed our approval.

But now he flew low over the Mississippi's murky waters, the wheels of his plane almost touching the rippled surface, our hearts beating wildly in fear that he would crash to a watery end, all of us screaming implorations, but he maintained a steady few inches above the water; then he did the impossible—a sight forever etched in a seven-year-old's memory—right before our eyes, he flew the plane *under* the Eads Bridge, under the moving bridge traffic, the wheels dipping into the water to get low enough, and then he zoomed up above us, the Mississippi water dripping from the wheels and all of us cheering as we had never cheered before.

So, as far as I was concerned, Lindbergh was the Messiah. When I was in high school, I read his book, *We,* and for me there was no hero within light-years of him. Now in 1940, Lindbergh had emerged as one of the leaders of the America First movement, which was fanatically dedicated to keeping us out of any foreign involvement. His very participation in America First was persuasive, for Lindy was noted for his shy, withdrawn personality, especially since the kidnap-murder of his infant son in 1932. But Lindbergh had gone to Germany as a guest of the Hitler government, he had personally observed the military machines and soldiers of the Reich, and he was now carrying the word to the American people that the Nazis were invincible, that their power could never be challenged, and that it would be folly even to consider a military confrontation with the German war machine. I never doubted for a second that Colonel Lindbergh's word was law in Washington and that the government would follow his advice. This incipient draft for which I was registering was, I thought, a formality undertaken for psychological effect and nothing more.

There were other reasons why I didn't take registering for the draft seriously. I had graduated from Washington University Law School (I had entered college at age fifteen) and had started to practice with the firm of Taylor, Mayer, Shifrin & Willer. The general feeling was that even if mobilization did become a reality, lawyers would be part of the elite group that draft boards would exempt. (Like being called for jury duty and then excused when the judge discovered you were a lawyer.)

My negative attitude toward being drafted had nothing to do with my feelings about what was happening in Europe. The Nazi atrocities against the Jews and the brutal conquests of relatively defenseless countries had disgusted and angered me—but in the Midwest we were resigned to the fact that Europe now belonged to Hitler (England was being subjected to a relentlessly devastating attack by air and capitulation seemed inevitable) and that we could do nothing about that militarily, that all we could do would be to oppose Hitler as an economic and political force in the world. However, if there had been indications that Hitler was preparing to attack the United States I most certainly would have rushed into uniform.

But the underlying fact was that I had been born and raised in a rare period of total global peace. During the twenties and thirties not a single military engagement had occurred anywhere in the world—an unprecedented period of warlessness—and military activity, to my generation, was unknown. The United States maintained a very small, badly equipped, obsolete army, and the peacetime soldier was held in low esteem, an object of ridicule who was frequently seen in the seamier sections of our cities, drunk, unruly, often panhandling—an inept, poorly educated, badly paid individual, shunned, an outcast. Ex-convicts, hoboes, and rummies were among those taken into the ranks—how else to fill even those meager quotas?—and one looked upon entering the army as one would contemplate a prison term among the inmates of Sing Sing.

I have said that war was alien to my generation, but nevertheless I am humiliated to recall my initial reaction when I read the first headlines on Hitler's invasion of Poland. There was a large map on the front page of the *St. Louis Post-Dispatch* showing the advance of the invading Nazis, and as I studied that map I felt a surge of what I confess was a pronounced excitement. In prelaw I had been a history major, which meant that much of my academic life had been spent studying wars. I don't know about today's history books, but certainly in those days historical events were mostly wars and important historical figures were the men who fought them. A history book was one long compendium of battles and conquests. As a result of my studies, I had perforce become quite knowledgeable about all the wars fought since the Crusades, but what I had studied was a dry, remote, hearsay chronicle of events; when I realized that Germany had actually started war, the history student in me was pleased that I would finally have a chance to follow a war in detail, to experience for myself that which had been remote.

My draft number was halfway down on the national list, so it wasn't until February 1941 that I received a letter from the president of the United States that began, "Greeting: You are hereby ordered to report for induction into the armed forces of the United States . . ." I requested a deferment on the grounds that my professional services were needed on behalf of beleaguered clients. Without so much as a hearing, my draft board perfunctorily granted me a six-month postponement. In actual fact I had no clients of my own. As low man on the Taylor, Mayer, Shifrin & Willer totem pole, my functions consisted of performing the flunky duties that traditionally befell a firm's neophyte barrister. But I couldn't see that there was a crying need for my induction as a buck private into the United States Army. As a boy I had never had any soldier fantasies, not even cowboy-Indian fantasies, and as an adult I was decidedly not the military type. In fact, I was a pacifist.

In the thirties, people openly and forcefully identified their beliefs: agnostic, atheist, isolationist, freethinker, pacifist. I was not outspoken about my beliefs but I identified with the pacifists, a word that is virtually obsolete now. At Washington University, aside from the handful of men in ROTC and the twenty or so women who comprised the Sharpshooters, an all-girls rifle club, most of the students on campus, it seemed to me, were pacifists. When I was editor of the university's literary magazine, *The Eliot,* I devoted an entire issue to pacifism. That a pacifist, as I was, should have felt a rise of excitement over Hitler's invasion of Poland is something that I now look back upon in total bafflement.

By the time my six-month deferment expired, in August 1941, world conditions had changed somewhat and so had my lawyering status. The production of military supplies and weapons in the United States had fallen far behind demand, and there weren't enough military installations to house and train even those men who had already entered service. As for the world situation, it was less grim—England had withstood the Luftwaffe and the guided missiles, and the English air force was even mounting a few retaliatory sorties of its own. President Roosevelt had maneuvered the Congress into establishing lend-lease as a means of supplying ships and supplies to our allies, and Hitler was in a relatively quiescent state, regrouping after his frustrated assault on the Soviet Union.

So it seemed to me there was even less urgency for me to enter the army than there had been six months before. Besides, I was in the midst of a criminal proceeding that involved a defendant, my client, who, if found guilty, would go to the electric chair. And in those days when one was sentenced to die in the electric chair, that's where, in all likelihood, one wound up.

My firm did not handle criminal litigation but in this case I had been appointed by the court. To defend indigent people accused of crimes who could not afford a lawyer, judges in the criminal courts picked lawyers at random from the bottom of the rolls of the bar association—in other words, from among the young, inexperienced lawyers who had just passed their bars and been admitted to practice. In this manner I had been directed (court-appointed lawyers had no choice in the matter) to take on the defense of one Steve R. Cysmanski. I went to the city jail where Mr. Cysmanski was being held without bail. The Cysmanski file and Cysmanski arrived at about the same time. I was seated in the lawyers' room, at a wooden desk behind a foot-high divider, and had just opened the file when the elevator slowly rose into view from the cell blocks below. Out stepped a guard, followed by a six-foot-eight-inch Frankenstein's monster dressed in gray jail pants and a dirty undershirt, over the top of which cascaded a Niagara of ominous chest hair. I presumed that this huge object hulking toward me was Cysmanski and rose to greet him as he approached, but he did not shake hands or acknowledge me. He sat down, leaned across the barrier, and said in a guttural, heavily accented voice, "This whole thing's a crock of shit."

"Mr. Cysmanski," I said, looking at the open file, "I have not had a chance . . ."

"Little whore doin' it for two bits a throw with every little fart in the neighborhood . . ." I was reading the indictment as fast as I could. " . . . takes after her whore mother . . . rape—ha! I don't no rape her—she just mad I don't give her money she want . . ."

As I quickly read, I could feel a distinct icy flow starting at my coccyx and moving up my spinal column toward the base of my skull. This was my first litigation, my first criminal proceeding, and what was the case? A father charged with the statutory rape of his fourteen-year-old daughter on not one, but eleven separate and documented occasions; in the state of Missouri, statutory rape carried a *mandatory* death sentence. Cysmanski was a steelworker who lived in one room in a boardinghouse with his daughter and his nine-year-old son. The mother was a streetwalker who, after slim pickings on the streets of St. Louis, had left the family circle the previous year to return to her original and more lucrative beat in downtown Milwaukee. Cysmanski, the indictment charged, followed a pattern of Saturday afternoon intercourse with his daughter (referred to as Saturday "rapes" in the file); the alleged pattern was that the son was sent out of the room at one o'clock while Cysmanski got in bed with his daughter, after which Cysmanski gave her fifty cents to take her brother and herself to a double feature at the neighborhood movie. There were detailed statements in the file by the daughter, the son, the landlady, and a quartet of social workers. The daughter was currently being cared for by nuns in the House of Good Shepherds, and the son had been placed temporarily in an orphanage.

When I cited these various indictments to Cysmanski, he became enraged. He roared a couple of expletives and pounded his flat hand on the table so hard I thought the walls would come down. So did the two floor guards who came running. "She is tramp, I tell you! I do nothing, nothing, NOTHING! She want a raise to one dollar and that is why she call the social worker and make all this troubles. Is blackmail—is for the one dollar. Two-bit little whore think she worth one dollar!"

In response to my request for another deferment, this time I was summoned to appear before my draft board. Ten middle-aged men, eight with paunches, six with glasses, all wearing neckties, behind a long wooden table, one folding chair facing the table for me to sit on. I described my involvement in the Cysmanski case to the board, and pointed out that although I had tried every which way to induce Cysmanski to plead guilty and to let me plea-bargain for him with the prosecuting attorney's office (the prosecutor had indicated he might consent to five years), Cysmanski was adamant in maintaining his innocence and rejecting any kind of deal involving admitted guilt. Actually, what Cysmanski had said was, "Me cop a plea? You crazy or something?! Wait I tell the jury—they see Cysmanski good honest fellow, hard of work, not guilty. Then afterwards, that little whore, that liar, that chippie from her mother, she better watch out. Oh, I get my hands on her! I break her everything!" But I didn't go into detail with the draft board.

What I did tell the board was that I was in the midst of preparing for Cysmanski's trial and I asked for another six months so that my client would be properly represented. The gentlemen of the draft board were very interested in some of the gamier details of the case and asked quite a few questions that had nothing to do with my draft status. Two days later, notification of another six-month deferment came in the mail. I wouldn't have to deal with my military fate again until February of 1942, and by then the war would very likely be over.

I worked hard preparing for Cysmanski's trial. My investigation disclosed that his daughter, a ripe, robust fourteen-year-old who looked five years older, was indeed the neighborhood chippie, doing it in the bushes with kids on the block for two bits a throw, but that was no legal solace for Cysmanski. I knew there would inevitably be a verdict of guilty which I would appeal, and since appeals took a year or more to be heard and decided, I felt it might be allowable grounds for a further draft postponement.

But after the jury was impaneled, the prosecuting attorney made an impassioned opening statement to the jurors, predominantly women, demanding that Cysmanski burn in the electric chair for his dastardly crime, and so well did he lard it on that

Cysmanski caved in, grabbing my arm, and in a strong voice shouted: "Cop the plea! Cop the plea!"

I asked for a recess and conferred with the prosecuting attorney, but since the trial had already started, he upped the ante to ten years, which Cysmanski eagerly embraced.

# Two

An unforeseen event undid my expectation that I would not be drafted, the Japanese assault on Pearl Harbor destroying forever the American delusion that the United States was a secure island, uninvolved with the rest of the world.

After Roosevelt declared war on Japan, I knew that there would be no more deferments, nor did I want any. But with only two months' leeway until my February induction date, it was now imperative to expeditiously choose a branch of service that would accept me as an officer. It never occurred to me that I was not one of the elite. I had completed six years of university, capped by graduating law school with a doctor of law degree. During my undergraduate career I had consistently been on the dean's list, and had been captain of the debating team, editor of the campus literary magazine, columnist for the student newspaper, playwright of student productions, on the editorial board of the law quarterly, on several athletic teams, president of various student organizations—in short, a man for all campus seasons. This inflated self-perception led me to expect that the military would be impressed with my credentials and let me pick and choose where and how I would fight for my country. I had two months to arrange for a commission—in my naive estimation, plenty of time.

I first applied to the Judge Advocate General for a direct commission as a second lieutenant, figuring that I could move on to a more combative branch once I received my commission. The Judge Advocate had a recruiting program that offered direct commissions to lawyers who, after a six-week indoctrination course, would perform legal functions for the various branches of the service. To my dismay, the Judge Advocate swiftly and unequivocally rejected my application. Young lawyers, who were applying in droves to beat the due date of their draft numbers, did not rate with the recruiters of the Judge Advocate, who were looking for older, experienced barristers. Actually, I was relieved by this rejection, for I much more identified with the pilots, foreign legionnaires, and storm-whipped bridge officers of hundreds of films I had watched at the neighborhood movie houses. To be honest about it, all those history books I had studied had had no real emotional impact on me, but Hollywood's schmaltzy versions of history, studded with such glamorous war heroes as the devil-may-care flying ace, the intrepid submarine commander, the duty officer lashing himself to the wheel—this was the real stuff of war that had charged my imagination.

So now that the time had come to embark on my own military career, I chose the Hollywood war hero that I found glamorous above all—the naval combat pilot. I was particularly influenced in this choice by a movie I had seen (twice) in which Dick Powell performed heroic aerial acts while wearing an exquisite white tunic, gold-buttoned at the throat, epauletted, festooned with gold braid: Dick Powell in rocketing descent, on the attack, looking right and left, coolly firing his machine guns, then up and away, leaving in his wake a smoking enemy plane spiraling out of control, that white-and-gold uniform as crisp and romantic on landing as it was at the start of the film. I had never set foot in an airplane but in looking through the recruiting brochure of the Navy Air Corps (I had assembled every available piece of material on all the commissions being offered by all the services) I concluded that the uniform was reason enough for choosing them above their competition.

I sought out my friend, Myron Gollub, who was scheduled to be drafted about the same time I was, and reminded him what a favorable impression Dick Powell's uniform had made on us when we had seen the film.

"Wasn't Dick Powell."

"Who was it then?"

"Dunno. But not Dick Powell—he sings."

"Okay—Tyrone Power or whoever. Point is, we were knocked out by the uniform, weren't we?"

"You mean you're choosing the Navy Air Corps because of the uniform?" Myron asked. Or, rather, growled. Myron was short, dark, introverted, and built like a middleweight wrestler (which he had been in college), and when irritated, he actually growled. We had been friends for many years.

"I know that seems superficial," I said, "but no matter what we go into it's a gamble, so we may as well wind up in a terrific uniform."

"You ever been in a plane?"

"No."

"Neither have I."

"And we've never been on a ship or marched in formation or carried a gun."

"What makes you think we could learn to fly one of those things?"

"We can drive a car, can't we? They say flying a plane's not a whole lot different. Besides, the flight pay for naval combat pilots is the highest of all combat officers."

"Why's that?"

"I guess because you mostly fly off of aircraft carriers and landing on an aircraft carrier is tougher than landing on a concrete strip."

"Well, I like the uniform, all right, but I don't think I'm cut out to be a pilot."

"Look, Myron," I said, "didn't we say we'd try to go in together?"

"Yes, but you didn't say . . ."

"Why don't we at least go downtown and talk to the navy people . . ."

"Because it's a waste of time—I don't want to be a pilot, period."

"Now wait a minute, Mo—are you saying that you are going to desert me after we made this pact to go into service together and help each other out? What kind of a friend is that?"

Myron growled something incomprehensible.

"Okay, I'll go it alone, but what you don't realize is that we're in a serious situation. What are we going to join if not the Navy Air Corps?"

"Oh, I dunno—maybe I'll just let the draft take its course."

"And go in as a buck-ass private?" I was horrified. Myron was as much a college elitist as I was—a newly graduated lawyer and, as I recall, a Phi Beta Kappa who had been elected to the Order of the Coif in law school.

"Why not? The only things I've ever done are wrestle and study, neither of which makes me a hot prospect for the military. You want to know something? I'm so bad at marching and drilling and all that crap that I washed out of the Boy Scouts. I didn't even make Tenderfoot."

"But the air corps teaches you everything you have to know," I insisted. "We go to the flying school at Pensacola, I think, and by the time we graduate we'll be tooling around the sky like a couple of pigeons."

"You mean eagles."

"Yeah, eagles."

"I just don't feel it, Hotch."

"As a favor to me. *I* feel it—we just go down and talk to them. What have you got to lose? We might sink a Jap battleship or knock down some kamikazes—you and me—a couple of war heroes. Be a pal."

"Well . . ." The growl deepened.

The Navy Air Corps recruiter, a commodore, explained that there were only twelve openings in the next class of the Navy Air Corps, which, he said, was the most exclusive branch of all the services. "Even though a college degree is a prerequisite for applying," he said, "only one applicant in a hundred can pass the written exam, and of those only one in fifty can pass the physical. But there is nothing to compare with the prestige of being a naval flyer." He pressed a couple of application forms on us and Myron had to agree that with odds like those he had very little to fear from putting in his application along with mine.

Very shortly after we filed the applications we were summoned to take the written exam. It was not what you'd call an easy examination, but for a couple of guys who had recently taken the bar exams, it was duck soup. We were called for our physical. There were approximately sixty men in the group that had been assembled for the physical, about fifty of whom looked like varsity running backs. Then, as now, I stood five feet nine and tipped the scales at 150.

The physical, which took three hours, was administered by a dozen navy doctors; in the process, we were turned inside out and eliminations were made as members of the group failed to pass one or another of the rigid inspections to which we were subjected. Myron was ahead of me in line and had already completed his physical by the time I got to one of the last tests—depth perception. I was led into a long, narrow corridor of a room that was pitch-dark except for a spotlight that illuminated two vertical pegs, each attached to a wooden pole that ran the entire length of the room.

The doctor who had just examined my eyes and found them to be 20/20 positioned me at the end of the room opposite the lighted area. He told me to take the ends of the wooden poles, which were on runners, in my hands and try to align the two pegs.

I squinted down at the pegs—one green, the other red—and maneuvered the poles to get them abreast of each other. The doctor shook his head. He said they were a foot apart and that I should try again. This time they wound up two feet apart. He suggested I go down to the lighted area and study the pegs. But it didn't help. I must have tried ten times, never getting the pegs closer than within a foot of each other.

"Tell you what," the doctor said, "there are only eight of you left and we would like to induct all eight of you. Why don't you go to lunch and we'll try again this afternoon. It's probably just nervousness."

"Why is depth perception so important?" I asked.

"Because without it, you'd have trouble landing a plane on the deck of a carrier."

I found Myron sitting on a chair near the door, looking forlorn. He didn't see me as I approached because they had put dilation drops in his eyes before testing him for night perception. In the order of things, night perception was the last examination, and the applicants who passed that were signed up. As a result of the drops, Myron's vision was so fogged I had to lead him to the little restaurant where we had lunch.

"How come they didn't put drops in your eyes?" he asked me as I guided him up a curb.

"Well, there's a little hitch about my depth perception."

"You've signed up, haven't you?" There was a touch of panic in his voice.

"After lunch," I said, "when I've lined up those frigging sticks . . ."

That afternoon I spent two hours in the depth perception room, but no matter how hard I tried, I just couldn't get those damn pegs to meet. The doctor even arranged for me to practice. No dice. Myron and I parted like partners who had just lost a doubles match.

We went to the movies the night before he left for Pensacola, and afterwards we had a couple of beers. We took turns consoling one another—I was dejected at having lost this opportunity to wind up in the gold-and-white tunic, and he was dejected at having to embark on this perilous aviation journey all alone. I walked him home. We promised each other to stay in touch. After we had shaken hands and said good-bye and good luck, I stood there and watched him go up the steps and disappear into his house. I felt a penetrating sadness, a feeling that the young part of my life was ending. Myron and I had had many adolescent adventures together. We had been counselors together at a boys' summer camp; we had studied together and played sports together, double-dated and played in many a penny-nickel poker game. I had always felt protective about Myron. He was a morose character, glum and inclined to anticipate catastrophe or, at least, disappointment. His mother, recently dead, had had a long, agonizing battle with cancer. As I recall, his father had died long before that.

Myron had a good sense of humor, a dry, sardonic wit, and a resonant laugh, but there was not much joy in him, or if there was, it was an orphan unattached to the happenings in his life. He was not a masochist but he did not have the capacity to savor the little triumphs and occasional strokes of good luck that befell him. He was a fatalist in the truest sense of the word. That he had applied for the Navy Air Corps against his inclination and just to accommodate me, and then found himself going off without me, was, for Myron, an inevitable card dealt to him from the bottom of fate's deck. Remembering Myron as he was then, what is sharpest about him in my memory is his sigh. He was the only person my age I knew who sighed. He sighed often, a deep, mystical, wailing sound that escaped from him involuntarily. He was compassionate, intelligent, attractive, and articulate, qualities that should have nurtured a different ego. Instead, there was that mournful sigh, as if he bore some dark, tormenting secret that he was obligated to take to the grave.

That was Myron, and I grieved to see him go off by himself. He lived a lonely life and it would have been nice for him to have had company on this uncharted journey to Pensacola. I myself had lived a lonely and sometimes painful adolescence and, of all people, I should not have been the one who let Myron down.

My other close friend was Carroll Donohue, called Chris. He was Myron's opposite number, a tall, blond, fair-skinned, outgoing, ebullient Irishman. Chris had been two classes ahead of me in law school but we had cut many a campus caper together. When I was editor of the literary magazine, Chris was the business manager, a relation that often led us astray, like the time we rigged the vote for the magazine's campus queen so that a girl whom Chris had been trying to impress could win. Chris was a totally exuberant man who laughed infectiously, told outrageous jokes, and effortlessly ranked at the top of his law class.

We also had in common the fact that we were dirt poor. Chris had worked his way through school playing trumpet in a dance band, and somehow in the process had also helped support his ailing, widowed mother. I had financed myself through six years of college by working at a variety of jobs ranging from stacking books in the law library to impersonating Harpo Marx on the downtown streets of St. Louis as an advertisement for the latest Marx Brothers movie. I fully expected that someday Chris's Irish charm and exuberance coupled with his quick intelligence would make him an irresistible political force: perhaps governor of Missouri, or senator.

It was Chris to whom I turned for my next plan of attack on the military. I discussed it with him during a band break while he was playing in a small combo at the Chase Hotel. He too had been rejected by the Judge Advocate, and the draft board had refused to exempt him on the grounds that he was his mother's sole support. He was in the same fix I was.

What I proposed to him was that we both sign up for the navy's V-12 program; this was a program offered to college graduates whereby they trained at the Great Lakes Naval Academy for several months and emerged as ensign deck officers.

"Well, I don't know," Chris said. "I hadn't planned on joining the navy."

"Did you see Tyrone Power in that navy picture that came out last year?"

"No. But I saw the trailer—it wasn't Tyrone Power."

"Okay, Robert Young, whoever—go see it. You'll see why we've got to get into V-12."

"What will I see?"

"You'll see just about the niftiest uniform you ever set eyes on. The navy dress white, and the everyday dark blue with the gold ensign stripe on the sleeve. Low-key. Terrific."

"Yeah, maybe," Chris said, "but I think I'll just take my chances in the draft."

"In the draft! Peeling potatoes and scrubbing latrines—you realize that? Or maybe in a mud trench, going over the top while the officers . . ."

"That's the last war—with all the modern tanks and airplanes, you can forget all those trenches. Look what happened to the Maginot Line. You see too many movies."

"Listen, Chris, no matter what kind of war it is, it's the ordinary buck private who gets it in the ass. That's why they call him buck—they pass the buck all the way down from the top and it stops with him. You and I have always aimed high—why should this be any different?"

"Because you and I don't know a damn thing about the navy

or the infantry or anything else, that's why. We don't even know what the V-12 is, for God's sake—you ever been on a boat?"

"Not a . . . real boat."

"Neither have I. The sea's a complete mystery to me. Better I should be drafted and take my chances."

"Will you do me a favor?"

"You can dream about being on a boat out there in your fancy uniform thinking you're Errol Flynn, but the reality is it's a war and someone's gonna be shooting at you—to *kill* you, for God's sake—enemy battleships, U-boats, Luftwaffe—and when you're stuck on a boat, with all that stuff coming at you, there's no goddamn place to hide."

"Will you do me a favor? Just come down to the recruiting office with me and have a talk with the officer in charge."

"It's a waste of time."

"Please—what have you got to lose?"


Naval Recruiting for the V-12 program occupied an entire floor of the Bell Telephone Building at 1010 Pine Street. The written examination, considerably easier than the one for the Navy Air Corps, was followed by an interview conducted by a lieutenant whose simple questions were obviously designed to facilitate enrollment; as was the physical, which passed more than half of the applicants in our group. As Chris and I neared the end of the physical, I suffered a moment of dreadful anticipation that I would have again to face the ordeal of a depth perception test, but that wasn't on the agenda and Chris and I were told that we had both qualified and that we could now sign papers of enlistment. The recruitment officer shook our hands, and with heady euphoria I flourished my name across the document that made me a candidate for the rank of ensign in the navy of the United States of America. I stood proud, with my shoulders squared and a look of patriotic determination on my face.

Chris proposed that we have a celebratory lunch at the Boatman's, a restaurant where his law firm had a charge account (my salary at Taylor, Mayer, Shifrin & Willer was a beneficent $75 a month and Chris's was about the same), and, with a vista of dry martinis beckoning, we were starting out the door when a navy doctor, a captain, came into the room and called my name; he had my medical chart in his hand. He motioned me to an examining room where I stood at attention while he studied my chart.

"This almost slipped through," he said.

"Something wrong?" I asked, with a dry throat.

"Take off your shoes and socks," he said.

When I was barefooted, he asked me to step up on a stool that elevated me a few feet off the ground. He squatted and closely studied the bottoms of my feet. I desperately tried to slant my feet toward the outside, away from my insteps.

"Hotchner," he said, straightening up, "you're flat-footed."

"Well, it's true I don't have much of an arch . . ."

"You don't have *any* arch. You're flat as a pancake."

"But, Captain, this is the navy, isn't it? It isn't as if it's the infantry or marines where you have to . . ."

"The navy is harder on the feet than the infantry."

"You march in the navy?"

"As an ensign on a destroyer with its metal deck, on a pitching sea, it's worse on your feet than a twenty-mile hike. Even with good arches, we have a lot of pedal breakdown. Lucky we caught you here, else they would have washed you out when you got to the academy."

"But, Captain, my feet are strong as girders. I played all kinds of sports—tennis, basketball . . ."

"Mister, flat feet are not acceptable in the navy," he said in a tone of dismissal. He scribbled something across a piece of paper and handed it to me. "Give this to the desk officer on your way out."

Loathing my feet and the United States Navy, I reluctantly put on my socks and shoes and returned to the outer room where Chris was waiting for me.

"What's up?" he asked.

"You're not going to believe this, but . . ."

# Three

As it must have been for many of the young men of my generation, going into the military was the first time I had been away from home. (Actually, I had spent two summers as a counselor at a camp in the Ozarks but I don't count that as being out in the world, on my own.) Travel was not as easy in those days as it is now. The Depression still had its stranglehold on our lives and most families could barely pay for rent and food, let alone afford to travel. Certainly not my family. For much of my young life we were fortunate to eat one meal a day, and as for rent, my father took advantage of a practice whereby landlords, strapped with debts and vacancies, would offer several months of rent-free concessions as an inducement to the signing of a two-year lease. My father would sign such a lease, but when the rent-free period ended, he would stall the landlord for a few additional months and then make us surreptitiously pack our meager belongings and steal away in the dead of night. Which accounts for the fact that I attended eleven different grammar schools in various sections of St. Louis, and a variety of high schools.

But by the time I entered Washington University, my mother had found employment as a secretary and we were living at a constant address, paying rent and eating more or less regularly. I augmented my scholarship with campus jobs, one of which was working for Professor Theo Lentz of the psychology department, who operated a psychological testing laboratory. I was paid fifteen dollars a month to administer lengthy, detailed questionnaires that probed the intimate lives of the subjects, a study that predated Masters and Johnson in the sexual details it evinced.

By the time I finished law school, we were not only enjoying three meals a day but also occasional movies; such indulgences as travel and vacations, however, were still completely out of the question. So the prospect of going off to unknown military destinations became an insecure excitement. My mother mentioned giving me a going-away party but my father, displaying his usual tact, was outraged.

"And who's going to pay for it? You know what it costs? Coca-Cola, sandwiches, cake, maybe."

"I've saved up a little," my mother said.

"Then get shoes. Walking around with holes in the bottom, water gets in, snow gets in, you'll get pneumonia."

"I can get along."

My father turned to me. "You want a party? Your mother needs shoes—you want a party?"

My father had no job, no income, but he had the arrogance of a provider. Naturally, I did not have a going-away party, but if truth be told I really didn't want one. Most of my friends had already been drafted and what's more, we had never been able to afford a party, not for birthdays or graduations, not for my brother or myself, and at this late stage in the game it was not an event I hankered for.

Taylor, Mayer, Shifrin & Willer assured me that they would keep my place at the law office, but as I waited for the military bus at the city hall at 6 A.M. on Valentine's Day, 1942, I had a strong premonition that I would never return to Taylor, Mayer, Shifrin & Willer, or, for that matter, to St. Louis. It was not that I felt confident that I would have a future more appealing than my lowly niche at the law firm: quite the opposite, for having twice been rejected in my efforts to serve at the controls of a bomber or on the deck of a destroyer, I felt that the luck that had always rescued me had turned its back on me and consigned me to a dismal future. I simply felt that practicing law, now that I had had a whiff of it, would be more dismal than almost anything that the future might bring.

As the bus pulled away, my mother among a phalanx of mothers waving tearful good-byes, I felt no sense of anticipated adventure, only a glumness that matched the cold, damp interior of the bus. As the bus made its way down the dark, deserted streets, I thought about my father, who had not awakened to tell me good-bye. I thought about how "absent" he had always been, not literally, but as a father. We had never had a semblance of a father-son relationship, never went to a baseball game, had a picnic, hiked, played catch, none of those father-son things. He never tried to teach me to ride a bike or roller-skate, and his one attempt to tell me the facts of life, when I was twelve (by which time I already knew), was pathetic, something about the rooster and how the chicken lays an egg. There was very little positive about him. Mostly he concerned himself with ways to avoid responsibility, like his scam on the rent concessions with landlords. For his scam with the electric company, he performed a bypass operation long before the surgeons got around to it. My father's operation consisted of disconnecting the main electrical wire from the meter box and connecting it directly to the household line, bypassing the meter, which, of course, would not register the amount of electricity we used, thereby virtually wiping out our electric bill. There was inherent danger in this since he could have been electrocuted in the process, but he always managed to reconnect the line to the meter the day before the meter man came to read it. He took great pride in these accomplishments and often boasted about them, particularly the way he eluded being drafted in the First World War. He knew that his draft board was giving deferments to the husbands of pregnant women, and although my mother was not pregnant, my father somehow managed to produce a medical document that earned his deferment. He was quite proud of this feat, about which he often boasted while I was growing up; it evoked in me a feeling of shame, a humiliation for my father's cowardliness, and probably motivated my own driven desire to make my mark in combat, compensating somewhat for my father's shameful scam.

# FOUR

The induction center for the St. Louis area was Jefferson Barracks, an ancient installation which, from the rusty, paint-peeling, rickety look of it, had more than likely been built as an induction center for the Civil War. Thousands of us were run through an assembly line of PFCs who tossed us underwear, socks, pants, shirts, tunics, shoes, overcoats, caps, and other GI clothing, all of the sizes determined by a corporal who guessed at our dimensions. As we shuffled past him he called out a number, which was the size tossed to us as we moved down the line. Most of my things were too large, especially my shoes, but back at the barracks I was eventually able to barter myself into a uniform that was an approximate fit.

But there was no way to barter myself out of going to a huge Air Force reception center in Texas to which I was assigned along with several thousand other Jefferson Barracks inductees. The method of assignment—whether one went to the army, navy, or army air force—was probably determined by lottery or by the alphabet or some other system that only the Jefferson Barracks gurus could fathom. My assigned destination was the U.S. Army Air Force Technical Training Command's reception center at Sheppard Field, located near the town of Wichita Falls in the northernmost part of Texas at the Oklahoma border. It was the air force, all right, not the elite airborne air force but the grunts who would service the mess halls, latrines, grounds, hangars, motor pools, and other drudge areas of the hundreds of airfields that were being quickly constructed all over the country.

The reception areas, ill-suited for military use, were palmed off at hefty purchase sums by influential people who knew how to take advantage of the system. Thousands of men beyond draft age, long unemployed because of the Depression, found jobs building miles of wooden barracks, mess halls, infirmaries, post exchanges, movie theaters, and all the other structures that composed a reception center. Farmland became drill fields. Town dumps became supply depots. The slapdash buildings had cracks between the boards that invited blowing sand and icy winds into the barracks, and the roofs ran rivulets of water in rainstorms. There were no fans to combat the often intense heat of summer, and the inadequate furnaces were no match for the cold that knifed through the barracks' walls and windows.

The purpose of the reception centers was to outfit and give basic training to all recruits and then assign them to various air corps installations in the United States and around the world. Most recruits had absolutely no preparation or ability for the task at hand. It was possible to apply to specialized schools, such as radio, motor pool, and aircraft maintenance, but not until basic training and initial assignments were completed.

The metal cots in the Sheppard Field barracks were precisely two feet apart, three widely spaced hanging bulbs were the only illumination, and the hot water was in very short supply. When I drew Texas as my destination, I had expected mild weather, but this was northern Texas in February and it was no different from the brutal winter of St. Louis.

The morning after our arrival, my barracks was routed at 5 A.M. along with hundreds of other inductees and marched to a staging area where we formed lines and slowly shuffled forward in the predawn Texas dark, freezing our asses off and I don't mean figuratively. Those who had put on their GI overcoats were all right, but those like myself who wore only their tunics had no protection against the unobstructed surly wind that whipped across the open drill fields. There was not a tree, shrub, sagebrush, or cactus, not an animate or inanimate impediment to the wind for miles in every direction. Senator Morris Sheppard of Texas, chairman of the Military Affairs Committee, had boondoggled this miserable, worthless, sandy expanse into the huge complex that bore his name: six hundred acres with ten mess halls, hundreds of barracks, and a capacity of twenty-six thousand inductees, the entire installation having been hastily built from scratch in six months.

The line I was in stretched interminably across the drill field, looped around the mess hall, and disappeared behind the post exchange. Imperceptibly we were inching toward a huge hangar-type building on which appeared the simple sign: MEDICAL. It was now closing in on 6 A.M. We had been forbidden entrance into the mess hall so that, I suppose, breakfast would not contaminate the purity of the urine specimens we were about to deposit.

As we neared the entrance to the building, a corporal at the door ordered, "Drop your pants and your shorts." That's when those of us without overcoats were strafed by the wind-whipped sand. With my pants and shorts down to my ankles, the high-velocity sand made a pincushion of my butt. A huge, rawboned Ozarkian in front of me whined to the corporal, "Why cain't we bare ass when we gets inside?"

A master sergeant up the line, ominous stripes all over his sleeves, stomped over. "What's he say?"

"He wants to know why he can't wait to dump his pants till he gets inside," the corporal said.

The master sergeant wound up and kicked the Ozark GI squarely in the behind. "That's why," he said. The master sergeant then slowly glowered around at us to be sure we all got the message.

So there I stood in the Texas predawn, my pants on my shoe tops, trying to protect my genitalia with my shirttail and with the medical form that each of us was carrying. I felt demeaned to the point of anger. Sonsabitches! Don't they realize I don't belong here? I am an educated man. A.B., L.L.B. I can type. I debated Cambridge University. There was an article about me in the *St. Louis Post-Dispatch*. I'm a lawyer. I kept Cysmanski from the electric chair. Why have they tossed me down to the bottom of the pit like this? God knows I did everything I could to avoid this miserable fate and give my all to the Navy Air Corps or the V-12.

Sonsabitches!

Inside the door there was another corporal who kept saying, "Shake your ass. Move it. Shake your ass." Just beyond him was an elevated ramp. The GIs in front of me, trying to climb the three wooden stairs that led to the ramp, were tripping and falling all over the stairs because they were hog-tied by their pants. I eased my pants up to my knees and managed to get up the stairs without falling.

Sonsabitches!

At the top of the steps I found myself at the beginning of a long, wooden runway on which the assembly line of bare-assed GIs, slowly shuffling forward, were being examined. What stretched before me, as far as the eye could see, under blindingly bright illumination, was a mass short-arm inspection. Standing on each side of the runway were military doctors and orderlies. The elevated ramp put the GI penis at the doctor's eye level.

The first doctor I encountered poked a hernia-seeking finger beside my testicles and told me to cough. Twice. Marked my medical form. I moved on. The next doctor pushed his thumb into the liver area of my stomach. Two hard thrusts. Hurt. Marked my form. I moved to another doctor who put his icy fingers on my penis, pulled it up, side to side, examined the tip. Penis shrunk.

The doctor next to icy fingers said, "Jesus, look at this, Phil."

Phil looked, and so did I. The doctor had stripped back the foreskin on the penis of the GI next to me whom I recognized as Lamar Ottersby, one of the toughest of the rednecks in my barracks. There was a dirty, heavy crust all around the head of his penis, which the foreskin had covered.

"Don't any of you guys ever wash?" his doctor asked. "Just take a look at his." He pointed to my penis, which shrunk even more. "Now that's the way a penis should be."

Lamar looked contemptuously at my penis. I knew there would be hell to pay. My circumcised penis had already drawn a lot of derision from the Texas, Kansas, Ozarks, and Oklahoma backwoods types who populated my barracks. The luck of the draw. Tens of thousands of men pouring into Sheppard Field every week from the Pacific to the Mississippi and I wound up in a barracks where I was the only circumcised city boy among a concentration of fully sheathed, rednecked country boys.

"Move on down to Post Three," the doctor said to Lamar. "They'll strip that crust off there and disinfect you. How come you don't strip back and wash?"

"Because ah doan play with mahself lahk some people," Lamar said, glowering at me.

The doctor on the other side of me called out, "Clap!"

The penis he was examining had a white discharge coming out of the tip. An orderly came down the ramp and led the offending GI away. For the next twenty minutes or so while I was on the assembly line, there were quite a few calls of "Clap!"

Now they told us to back up, bend over, and spread our cheeks so that the doctors on the other side of the ramp could examine our anuses.

Sonsabitches!

The last section of the elevated ramp was devoted to gathering urine specimens in small glass bottles. An orderly admonished, "Don't piss it full." I was about to urinate in my bottle when a familiar voice whispered in my ear, "Hotch, I'm in a jam." It was Harry Greensfelder, whom I knew from the tennis team at Washington University. Sweat was running down Harry's face and he looked like he was in the third set of a tough match. He was clutching an empty urine bottle. He looked frightened.

"I can't piss," he whispered.

"What's wrong?"

"I've been trying like hell but I got this block I can't piss in public."

"Well, maybe they'll let you . . ."

"No, I asked but they just yelled at me. I can't even piss in urinals if someone's standing next to me. I've been here for ten minutes with my dick in this bottle."

I could see that Harry was on the point of cracking up. I looked around at the doctors and orderlies—they were all busy and the ramp was crowded with GIs pissing into bottles. I took Harry's bottle and quickly peed in it. Then I shut off and peed the rest of what I had in mine. I gave Harry his half-filled bottle.

"Hotch, I'll never forget that you did this for me," he said, oozing gratitude.

"You've got whatever I've got, Harry."

"You're a helluva friend," he said.

After the urine concession, the line moved down from the elevated ramp onto ground level. We were told to pull up our pants and take off our shirts. Shots in both arms—typhus, typhoid, yellow fever, tetanus, smallpox vaccination, all at one time. Then, finally, a blood sample, after which we put on our coats and were discharged into that cold, sand-filled wind. It was light now and greasy smells from the mess hall filled the air.

The directive simply said that as a result of recent GI physicals, "the Commanding General of Sheppard Field has determined that it is in the best interests of the Army Air Force that personnel be circumcised. Tyson's glands under the foreskin produce secretions that form a cheese-like substance known as smegma which emits a foul odor and breeds disease. In fact, smegma encourages penile cancer. Compliance with this directive will be on a voluntary basis, but as an incentive those complying will be given a three-day pass."

"Shit, man," Lamar Ottersby said, "little snip o' skin and we got us three days to raise hell. We get paid tomorrow and we could have us a high ol' time."

Our pay was twenty-one dollars a month, which was only seventy cents a day but it could buy a lot of hell in Wichita Falls, where a room in the hotel was two dollars a night. One after another, the rednecks signed up. Our barracks chief, Leroy Higgins, a slung-belly corporal who had been in the peacetime army for fifteen years (following his discharge from San Quentin for armed robbery), led the group to the infirmary. Higgins was an illiterate, sadistic, sour-faced man but he was disconcertingly pleasant and cheerful the morning he took the group to the infirmary. I was left alone in the barracks and, believe me, I was glad to see all of them go. After the incident during penis inspection, I had been given the nickname of "Short-arm"—the circumcisions of my tormentors should put an end to that, I thought.

I would have three blissful days without them. Without the blare of "You Are My Sunshine," "She'll Be Comin' 'Round the Mountain," and "Turkey in the Straw" coming from dozens of competing radios. Without farts, teeth-grindings, sour smells from food packages, belches, disgusting jokes, and latrine stenches that permeated the barracks.

The day after the group's departure, Higgins sent me to the infirmary ward with their medical records. It was a long, narrow ward, row upon row of hospital beds, each with a moaning GI lying on his back, no covers, his penis heavily bandaged. Bandaged penises to infinity.

"They can't stand the slightest pressure," the ward orderly explained, "like the touch of a sheet or pajamas—drives 'em crazy. Poor bastards, thought there was nothing to it—hell, circumcising an adult is fuckin' painful."

"That was a dirty trick," I said. "The army should have warned them about that."

The orderly smiled at me, and I felt silly for having said it.

The group returned to the barracks four days after their circumcisions. They were not very chipper and some of them complained that it still hurt too much to pee.

"All right, Corporal, here we are," Lamar Ottersby said to Higgins. "They really suckered us on this one but leastways we get our three-day passes."

"What three-day passes?"

"The ones we was promised for gettin' our dongs clipped."

"You've just *had* your three-day passes—in the infirmary," Higgins snarled. "Now let's scrub up this place, it's a real shit-hole."

In the days that followed, a lot of incoming GIs were similarly induced to get themselves circumcised, but none of the circumcised veterans ever spilled the beans. It remained a steadfast, silent conspiracy, and those who had so painfully lost their foreskins and their three-day passes got a measure of revenge out of watching the new lambs being led to the slaughter.

# Five

I have never known an isolation, a loneliness, like I experienced in my "home" barracks. After a few days of taunting me, the good old boys eventually lost interest in the peculiarities of a college-educated lawyer from the big city who read books without cartoons in them. I was an outsider, and although it was a blessing that they ignored me, it also meant I had no one with whom to share my misery, the dehumanizing effect of mass drilling (four thousand men at a time in the frigid wind toting heavy World War I Enfield rifles), catching kitchen duty (the dreaded white towel tied to the foot of your cot), and latrine duty (a form of irrational punishment inflicted by the lard-ass barracks chief). The massive quantities of inedible food, turned out by GI cooks who prepared stuff by the numbers from an army manual, added to the overall misery. When a food parcel from my mother did succeed in finding me it was confiscated by Slung-Belly Higgins on the dubious grounds that all GI food had to be screened.

Lying there on my cot under the naked overhead bulb that was too dim to read by and with a noisy crap game in progress, I often envied Myron and Chris as I imagined the glamorous training they were experiencing. I bitterly reflected on how close I had come to joining them, only to be undone at the last moment by my feet and my eyes.

There was only one place where one could escape the barracks and that was the PX (post exchange), a dreary barn where GIs could buy cigarettes and a disgusting brew called near beer or, more often, piss-beer. With Ernie Tubbs music blasting, cigarette smoke fogging the room (I did not smoke), and only a few crowd-

35

ed tables, it was not much of an alternative to my deadly barracks. WACs (Women's Auxiliary Corps) were beginning to arrive but they were stationed in a remote section of the field and kept apart from the men. There were no black GIs or Sheppard Field civilian personnel.

After four weeks of exhausting drill field exercises, boring kitchen duty, and a numbing existence in the barracks, I should have become an automaton, resigned to a military future as miserable as my present one. But I had survived bleakness at an early age by virtue of an unreasonable determination to overcome oppression, and that same determination kept me above despair in the limbo of believing that Something Would Happen, not specifically identified. Even though I was but a dot on the acres of drillscape GIs who filled the immense expanse of Sheppard Field, I would somehow, someway, emerge from that dismal underworld into the light. When I was twelve and living alone in a seedy hotel room in St. Louis, my mother in a sanitarium, my father traveling with his line of unsalable watches, my young brother farmed out to relatives in Keokuk, Iowa, and a sadistic bellhop hell-bent on locking me out of our room and confiscating our meager belongings because our rent hadn't been paid, I barricaded myself into that room with no thought of surrender, relying as I always had on divine intervention. I had survived numerous seemingly insurmountable situations, much the same as Pauline had survived her perils at the movie house on Saturday afternoons. Resignation was not in my nature, but after weeks of being battered by Sheppard Field it began to look as if my resilience would finally expire.

Then came a glimmer of hope, posted on the bulletin board at the PX: applications were being offered for admission to bombardier school. Bombardier! I applied immediately. Finally, a possible way out of that wasteland and a chance to get into *action*. My mind was immediately inflamed with heroic visions of me at the controls of a bombsight as my crew holds steady against the attacking Messerschmitts and I zero in on the munitions factory in Stuttgart, then bombs away! and Sergeant Hotchner scores a direct hit, the explosion below is tremendous, and we return to base, shooting down three or four Messerschmitts along the way.

Two days after I filled out the application, I was summoned to take the bombardier test along with—my spirits fell—several hundred other applicants. But I attacked the questions with confidence although I was on shaky ground dealing with mathematical equations, not one of my strong subjects. It was amazing how the prospect of becoming a bombardier lifted me from the miasma of oppression that had stifled me. I was like a prisoner with the sudden prospect of imminent parole.

Actual parole came even sooner than I expected as I experienced another of those aforementioned twists and turns, always unanticipated. A few days later—a particularly raw, stormy day, the wind-driven sand stinging my face as we marched interminably from one end of the vast drill field to the other—a jeep careened into our midst, disgorging a master sergeant with a bullhorn who bellowed for attention, immediately freezing all of us in our tracks. I heard him intone: "Private Hotchner, front and center! You are to report to command headquarters." I was too startled to respond immediately. My first reaction was that I was in serious trouble. Why else would I be singled out from three thousand drilling GIs and in such an imperious manner? I eased out of my rank and moved toward the jeep, fear stiffening my legs. The sergeant gestured me into the jeep; he was a bellicose fellow, and I knew better than to ask him why I was being summoned.

The command compound was off limits to GIs, so I was seeing the headquarters buildings for the first time. It was certainly not the kind of jerry-built contraption I was living in. The jeep jettisoned me in front of the administration complex, the master sergeant saying his first and only words of the drive, "Captain Young, Section A," and then tooling off.

By the time I practically tiptoed down the long corridor that faced me and located Section A and Captain Charles Young, I was convinced that I was going to be court-martialed for some crime I had unwittingly committed. Nothing could be more intimidating to a lowly GI than endless closed doors, all bearing the names of high-ranking officers. Drawing a deep breath, I tapped gently on the door marked "Public Relations, Capt. C. R. Young," and he responded with a military "Enter." In the office was a WAC, busy at a typewriter, and Captain Young, a tall, trim officer who was seated at a desk, absorbed in inspecting a classification card. I took what I thought was a military stance in front of him and saluted—correctly, I hoped. "Private Hotchner reporting, sir."

"Sit down," he said, his eyes concentrated on the card for what seemed an eternity. I began to feel uncomfortably warm, and my GI shirt collar precipitously tightened.

Finally, eternity ended and Captain Young spoke to me, not taking his eyes off the card. "You went to Washington University?"

"Yes, sir. Law school."

The GI classification card was an eight-by-ten yellow card that contained vital information, from birth onward, and it shadowed a GI everywhere he went. It was amazing how much information was contained on that two-sided card.

"Listed here is a musical." Captain Young looked up at me for the first time. "You did a musical?"

"You mean at college?"

"That's what we're talking about."

Although still puzzled by this interrogation, I was somewhat relieved that it seemed unlikely now that I was in any serious trouble.

"Yes, sir, there was a musical . . ."

Every year, as its sole function, the Quadrangle Club produced a campus musical that was the joint effort of the drama society, the glee club, the band, and the dance group. A contest was held for the best original book, music, and lyrics. Over the years there were numerous Quad Club members who went on to professional careers, like comedienne Mary Wickes and author Shepherd Mead (*How to Succeed in Business Without Really Trying*). I had submitted a winning script called *Down in Front* and had written lyrics for songs composed by musically inclined friends of mine. My script concerned a down-at-the-heels salesman who bamboozles his way into big-time prizefighting by transforming a large, dumb, inept bum into a heavyweight contender—a sophomoric spoof of the corrupt world of boxing. I was amazed that it had found its way onto my classification card.

"You wrote this show?"

"I wrote the book."

"What's the book?"

"The spoken part. And some of the lyrics."

"For the songs?"

"Yes, sir."

"But not the songs?"

"No, sir."

"We have a directive here from the Chief of Staff that every base in the U.S. has to celebrate 'I Am an American Day' with an original show in the nearest city, which, in our case, is Wichita Falls. Proceeds are to go to the Army Emergency Relief Fund to help the widows and orphans of men who have been killed in action."

"Well, Captain, sir, I don't think *Down in Front* would be a good idea for such an occasion."

"Did I ask your opinion, soldier?"

"No, sir."

"The fact is I don't give a damn about *Down in Front*. The directive says an *original* show—you know what that means, *original*?"

"Yes, sir."

"Then you know why you're here."

"Not exactly, sir."

"To write this goddamn musical. We've got two weeks to present our show and you are being detached from your squad so you can join a group in Barracks 224 that will put it on. So get your gear and report to Sergeant Dale Stout on the double."

"I'm to write a musical in two weeks?"

"No, in four days. It has to be performed in two weeks, but you'll stay around until it gets on."

"What's the show about?"

"How do I know? You're the writer."

"Yes, sir."

"Dismissed."

"But sir, I've applied for bombardier school and I don't want to miss out on that."

"Soldier," Captain Young said, "you're to write a musical comedy, and it better not be a bomb."

"Yes, sir."

"Dismissed."

"Yes, sir."

Write a musical comedy in four days? Better it should have been a court-martial.

# Six

Barracks 224 was teeming with GIs like myself, arriving with their barracks bags, all on a mission to assemble this instant musical. Sergeant Dale Stout, a pleasant, literate man, the opposite of Corporal Higgins, took me into a partitioned room that was crowded with GIs who were being interviewed by one Corporal Bob Sylva, a handsome, lithe man with prominent, sculptured eyebrows and a dazzling smile.

"Have you written shows?" he asked me.

"In college."

"And since then?"

"I'm a lawyer."

"Good God! They send me a venetian-blind salesman for the music and a lawyer for the book. Well at least there's—what's your name?" He turned to a partially bald GI whose hangdog face featured a scraggly mustache.

"Harry Ginther, sir."

"I'm a corporal, not a sir. Harry here is a professional writer who is a ghostwriter for Jack Benny. But I'd like to have a choice, so let's see what each of you can turn out in four days."

That simplified things for me. Just write something soporific that would guarantee that I'd finish second to Ginther. So I outlined a preposterous script about a couple of GIs who conspire to smuggle a gorgeous girl, who's the general's daughter, into Sheppard Field secreted in a barracks bag so she can be with her true love. I mixed in a couple of goofy enlisted men, gave them lines guaranteed not to be funny, added a pompous major and some stupid MPs, and felt assured that my career as a heroic bombardier was looking good.

Ginther and I were sequestered in separate cubicles with type-writers and reams of paper. I zipped through my offering in three days, not bothering to rewrite anything or even reread it. I enjoyed the arrogance of being a surefire loser.

On the morning of the fourth day, Sylva came into my cubical with a limp script in his hand and a sick look on his face.

"Ginther . . . Ginther . . ." he practically sobbed, "Ginther . . . it's about . . . it's about this GI who falls in love with a cow. A purple cow. Please, God, help me." He picked up my script, which, in keeping with my corny book, was called *Three Dots with a Dash,* Morse code for *v,* for "victory."

"There's something fresh and funny about a guy and a cow," I said, desperately trying to lobby for Ginther. "We can think of lots of cow jokes and we could get two guys in a cow outfit . . ."

But Sylva wasn't listening. He was reading my script and *enjoying* it. Laughing. Identifying places for dance numbers and songs. When he finished reading it, he was giddy with pleasure and rushed out to tell everyone that we were on our way. I was dismayed. I had tried my best to write a bad script and I had failed. But then again, if my bombardier papers came through, I didn't have to stick around—my work was finished. I consoled myself with that possibility until that afternoon when Sylva announced that we would have a reading of the script so he could hear it before he cast the parts. He asked me to read the part of Jeep, a wiseass GI in charge of the smuggling operation.

Incomprehensibly, the script came across as lively and occasionally funny and not nearly as sappy as I had tried to make it. There was a discussion about what the songs should be and where they should go; Sylva blocked out the dances he would create. He had been a choreographer at the MGM Studio in Hollywood and with the Theatre Guild in New York, and he had also danced with the San Francisco Opera Ballet. Most of the men Captain Young had selected on the basis of their classification cards had professional backgrounds, so what was eventually assembled on the two floors of Barracks 224 were eighteen singers who would comprise the men's chorus and twenty musicians for the orchestra, GIs who had played in major symphony orchestras, swing bands like Tommy Dorsey's, and small-town orchestras. After a heated debate monitored by Captain Young, it was decided that the show's dancing chorus would consist of real, live Texas beauties and not a bevy of hairy-legged soldiers with balloons under their dresses.

That done, Sylva announced that as far as the performers were concerned there wasn't time for auditions so he would cast the show from the GIs already assembled, whereupon he began to distribute the scripts, which had by now been mimeographed. He handed me one. "You're Jeep," he said. "You were a terrific read."

"I'm sorry," I said, not taking the script, "but I've been accepted for bombardier school and I can't tie myself up with . . ."

Captain Young, who was sitting opposite me, was instantly in my face. "Soldier," he said emphatically, "this is an order. Pick up that goddamn script. We tell *you*, you don't tell us. Clear?"

"Yes sir," I said, hurriedly taking the script. "I just thought that as a bombardier . . ."

"Just don't bomb out when you get on stage." Everyone laughed, except me.

The part of my sidekick in the musical had been read by Jack Thomas, a tall, easygoing private who had been chosen to compose the songs for the show. He was also assigned a role, and the two of us were put in charge of arranging an audition in the town of Wichita Falls for girls to try out for the dancing chorus. The Wichita Falls newspaper ran an announcement about the audition, which was to be held in the ballroom of the local hotel. The morning of the audition, a serpentine line of aspiring girls wound around the hotel and, after our long isolation, it was very pleasurable for Jack and me to watch them cavort in tap shoes and ballet slippers for Sylva and his cronies. The eighteen who were chosen would certainly give the show, as Jack said, a pulchritudinous look.

Although his occupation was selling venetian blinds, Jack had written songs for amateur productions in Philadelphia and had appeared on *Major Bowes' Amateur Hour,* a network radio show, singing one of his compositions. His songs for *Three Dots with a Dash* were tuneful and witty, especially one I was to sing, "Don't Get Us Wrong, We Love the Army." I had acted in a couple of college productions but I'd never sung on a stage or anywhere else. I'm not even a shower singer. But by now I knew better than to protest; in the army if you're told to sing, you sing. It was not tantamount to having to attack a machine-gun emplacement, but having to sing in front of fifteen hundred people in the Wichita Falls auditorium was pretty close.

A few days before the opening performance, Jack came to me with a worried look on his face. He sat down at the piano and played something called "From the Lonely One to the Only One," cornball words and music, certainly unlike his other stuff.

"What's that?" I asked.

"Our new hit song."

"Our what?"

"You've got to find a place for it."

"Oh no I don't."

"Oh yes you do. It was composed by the general's wife, who fancies herself a successor to Richard Rodgers."

The part we were not able to cast was Flavia, the gorgeous girl who is smuggled into the barracks. She had to sing (somewhat) and act (somewhat) and dazzle the audience. None of the audition dancers qualified. But in the drugstore adjoining the hotel, where Jack and I went to make a few purchases, we found a perfect

Flavia behind the cosmetic counter, a tall, voluptuous seventeen-year-old with long black hair and seductive black eyes. Her name was Lynn Baggett and her father, who was behind the prescription counter, owned the drugstore. It took some persuasion to get druggist Baggett's permission (Lynn was obviously dad's sheltered treasure), but he finally acquiesced when Captain Young appointed a pair of chaperons for rehearsals, the mothers of two of the dancers.

Even though we rehearsed eighteen hours a day, seven days a week, fourteen days was an impossibly brief time to mount a musical, even a slapdash GI production for the simple folks of Wichita Falls. What saved us was the experienced professionalism of many of the performers, especially the orchestra, which, without benefit of orchestrations that could have taken weeks to prepare, was able to extemporize arrangements that had the exuberance of spontaneity.

For my part, as the pivotal comedian of the show, I received much-needed help by borrowing routines from the leading comics of the day—the slow-paced delivery of Jack Benny, the way Eddie Cantor skipped through a song, the scowling curmudgeonliness of W. C. Fields, even the famous oral-punctuation routine of Victor Borge, which I adapted to the reading of the general orders when challenged by an MP. Jack adjusted the range of my songs (I wasn't Johnny One-Note but damn near) and he wrote a couple of special-material songs for himself that allowed him to show off his nimbleness with a lyric.

Our main problem was the clang of warring egos, but Captain Young patrolled the rehearsal hall, putting out brushfires before they could spread. On days when his teeth weren't bothering him, Captain Young could be adroitly conciliatory toward ego-combatants, but when he had a toothache, which was more often than not, he dealt with miscreants ruthlessly, even to the point of banishing a few petulant cast members back to the drill field.

The fact of the matter was that Captain Young had a pathological fear of dentists and would rather endure a throbbing toothache than face a dentist's drill. He feared the dentist as Dracula feared the dawn. By studying his teeth in the mirror, Young had identified six major cavities; his father was a coal miner in Appalachia, where shafts were numbered, so to Captain Young a hole in the tooth was like a hole in the ground. On days when he was swallowing aspirins to alleviate the pain, he would announce that number two or number five was "acting up and I'm telling you now, nobody better fuck with me."

Of course, with only two weeks of rehearsal and performers that included a lawyer (me), a salesman, a cartoonist, a radio writer, two jugglers, and a druggist's daughter plus an untried orchestra, the show should have been a fiasco but it somehow overcame its deficiencies (which might have been the source of its charm) and landed with the Wichita Falls audience. I sang my two comedy numbers approximately on key and, buoyed by the audience's enthusiastic laughter, I felt pretty good about my performance and about the dumb book I had written. I would take off for bombardier school on Monday with good vibes from the many curtain calls and the knowledge that we had raised a goodly amount for the relief fund.

Saturday night's performance was attended by General J. E. Fickle (his true name, I swear it) and his wife. General Fickle's major accomplishment was that in 1910 he demonstrated how a rifle could be fired from an airplane. After the performance, the general gathered the cast and crew on stage and told us how proud he and Mrs. Fickle were of our production (and her song, of course). He said that such exquisite music, dancing, and GI humor were too good to be abandoned, so he had therefore instructed his staff to make arrangements for the show immediately to tour through all the states under his command: Texas, Oklahoma, Kansas . . .

I couldn't believe what I was hearing. Could I get Captain Young to listen to reason? I could offer to rehearse someone to replace me—but how could I if I had to leave on Monday? Okay, purple-cow Ginther wasn't too swift and he was about as funny as a vat full of GI mashed potatoes, but he knew the part and he could step in. I couldn't locate Captain Young, who had already left for the bar of the officer's club, but the following day, before I could talk to him, I received orders detaching me from Sheppard Field for an indefinite period of time and placing me in a special traveling unit under Captain Young's command.

"Captain Young, sir," I said, "about these showbiz orders, I received this previous directive to report to bombardier school so I won't be able to go on this tour, sir."

Just my luck, Captain Young was being tormented by number three and he looked at me like I was mold that he had to scrape off a head of cheese. "Hotchner," he seethed, "for some incomprehensible reason the audience thinks your performance is funny. General Fickle and Mrs. Fickle think you're funny. But I personally don't see anything amusing about you and your damn bombardier school, and if I hear another peep out of you, you're going to lose privileges."

"But, sir, what about these orders?"

"Wipe your ass with them."

"Yes, sir."

# SEVEN

The performers and support staff, a hundred strong, traveled in a fleet of army trucks preceded by staff cars carrying the chorus girls, the two chaperons, and Captain Young. There was also a special staff car for Sylva and three of his privileged henchmen. The rest of us bounced along on the hard, side-facing wooden seats of the trucks.

Our opening performance was to take place in the Will Rogers Memorial Auditorium in Fort Worth. We were all to be quartered on two floors of one of the better hotels, men on one floor, women on the other.

"There's going to be some kind of stampede up to the girls' floor after the show," I said to Jack Thomas. (There were sixty GI performers and only seventeen girls.) He gave me a look.

"Why the look?"

"You St. Louis guys are not very swift, are you?" was all he said.

Immediately after the performance a reception was to be given for the cast by the Junior League of Fort Worth. After that afternoon's dress rehearsal, Captain Young assembled the cast and admonished them to be on their best behavior since the league represented the upper crust of Fort Worth society. "Especially you, LaDorace." The dancing chorus was a mixed bag of "seasoned" Texas girls and naive innocents, the former with professional experience, the latter fresh out of dance class. LaDorace Dobson was definitely seasoned, an uninhibited swinger with dyed red hair and a rambunctious dedication to having a good time. She was also the best dancer in the chorus. Her closest friend, Dorothea, also "seasoned," was the most attractive chorine.

We were all apprehensive about how the large, sophisticated Fort Worth audience would receive us, but after the tumultuous reaction to our opening number, "The Hut-Hoot-Heet-Four Blues," sung by the men's chorus, we knew we had nothing to worry about. The following day the *Fort Worth Star-Telegram* headline was: "Sheppard Field Show Lays 'Em in the Aisles."

The young ladies of the Junior League all seemed to wear black dresses, pearls, white gloves, and patent leather shoes. They were gracious and our cast appeared to be on good behavior. Drinks were served by gloved waiters who also passed around a variety of fancy hors d'oeuvres the likes of which most of us had never encountered. I happened to walk by LaDorace as a platter of asparagus was being offered to her. In an accent that she doubtless assumed was upper-class, she was saying, "Asparagus? Thank you, no—it makes me piss stink."

When we returned to the hotel in buses that had been provided for us, what I had thought might happen didn't. The girls retired to their floor, and a considerable number of the men went off in a group to a room on the men's floor. When I went to my room, which I was sharing with Jack, the phone was ringing. It was LaDorace.

"Want to come up? Dorothea and I are in 406. Jack's here and we have a bottle of Southern Comfort courtesy of the Junior League."

"You won it as a door prize?"

"Something like that."

Now I knew why Jack had given me that look. It had not crossed my mind that homosexuals might be in uniform. In fact, the only homosexuals that I had been aware of while I lived in St. Louis were Louis Triefenbach and his cousin Thomas Lanier Williams. When I was editor of the Washington University literary magazine, *The Eliot,* Triefenbach was on the staff. A tiny, impeccable fellow who wore lavender shirts with white collars and tattersall vests, he occasionally submitted poems written by his cousin, who was also a student but who never came to the office.

Here, from my old *Eliots*, are a few of those poems written by Tom Williams in his college days, before he adopted the sobriquet of Tennessee:

*Recollection*

It was a steep hill that you went down,
Calling back to me,
Saying that you would be only a little while.
I waited longer than that.
The little grasses continued to stir in the wind
And the wind grew colder.

I looked across the deep valley
And saw the afternoon sun
Was yellow as lemon upon the dark pines,
And elsewhere pools of cool shadow
Crept down from the hills like stains of dark water
Widening slowly as the sunlight dimmed . . .

Someone called I think.
I do not remember clearly.
I only know that a long time afterwards
I rose from the grass
And walked slowly back down the path by which we had come,
The small, winding path,
And noted, here and there, your footprints,
Pointing upwards, narrow and light.

*Sonnet for Pygmalion*

For you, Pygmalion, no silver-bought
Woman of Cyprus with kohl-darkened eyes!
For you, Pygmalion, a vision caught
In its first blinding moment of surprise
And therein crystallized: no less than this:

Perfection carved by your own hand from stone,
The lips forever lifted toward the kiss,
The breast immutable and still unknown!

And so think twice: in making her alive
You stain her with the dust of time and change,
While you should have, in taking stone to wive,
Her loveliness forever new and strange,
Her palm a chalice and her lifted face
A fire, a sacrament, an altar place!

*Mummer's Rhyme*

Put away the painted masque
    Of poet or of clown,
The judge's wig, the warrior's casque,
    And ring the curtains down!
Some things were said in earnest and
    Some things were said in jest:
The princess had the whitest hand,
    The harlot's heart was best!
The prophet shouted loud and long—
    Who knows what he was saying?
The blindman starved amidst a throng
    Of honest people praying . . .
Now hang the masque upon the wall
    And ring the curtains down!
For shadows fall upon the hall
    And silence on the town!

As I said, Williams never came to the *Eliot*'s office, only his poems as couriered by Triefenbach. But one semester I encountered
Williams himself in a course in playwriting I took from a splendid
teacher, Professor William G. B. Carson, who, for our final grade,
required the writing of an original one-act play. Three of these
plays would be selected for production in the campus theater be-

fore a panel of drama critics from the *St. Louis Post-Dispatch*, the *St. Louis Globe-Democrat*, and the *Chicago Herald Tribune*, with the winning playwright awarded a plaque and fifty dollars in cash.

The exercises that Williams wrote for the playwriting class were deft, touching, fragile exchanges between an eccentric St. Louis mother and her slightly crippled, homebound daughter. My exercises were campus farce about a beleaguered student who wrote a gossip column for the school newspaper. I knew in my heart that my gossip columnist didn't stand a chance against Williams's mother and daughter.

But when the time came to submit our full one-acters, I was shocked that Williams had totally abandoned the characters he had been developing and instead submitted a play called *Me, Vashya!*, which was about an egomaniac munitions czar who sat in his office with the map of the world at his back, deciding where on earth to foment war to the benefit of his munitions factory. It was melodramatic, bombastic, and silly, based on a subject Williams knew nothing about, and it was not selected as one of the three plays to be produced. Williams was so outraged at this rebuff that he abandoned Washington University in the middle of the term and transferred to the University of Iowa, where the redoubtable Professor George Pierce Baker was head of the drama department. Later, Williams repeated this bizarre behavior when he first tackled the professional stage. His initial play, *Battle of Angels,* was a melodrama that folded in Boston, but then, righting himself, Williams wrote *The Glass Menagerie,* which finally made use of all those exercises he wrote in Professor Carson's class. I once asked Professor Carson why he thought Williams had switched away from the tender sketches he was writing. "He's a very sensitive man," Carson said, "who tried to go beyond the bounds of his considerable talent and invade a macho sensibility that was foreign to him."

In addition to my rather shocking discovery that there was a homosexual presence in the Air Force, I was becoming aware of how the war was affecting the heretofore submissive attitude of women. They were now performing jobs that had been the exclusive province of males and they were earning the kind of money that enabled them to determine where they would go, with whom they would go, and how they would go. The liberation of women was in full cry as the war was getting under way. The popular song "Rosie the Riveter" was its anthem. In uniform, in the factories, in the offices now devoid of males, women were in charge of their own destinies. For the first time, they asked men for dates and they had sex when they wanted to. They changed the way they dressed, spent much less time in the kitchen, and entrusted their kids to care centers so they could work.

The day after LaDorace invited me to her Southern Comfort party, Dorothea took me aside during afternoon rehearsal. Dorothea was the only pure platinum blonde I ever knew then or now, as striking, in her way, as Jean Harlow, although not as pretty. "Listen," she said, "I've been thinking—we get along pretty good, don't we?"

"Well, yes."

"So I thought we'd just be with each other." She had a dancer's way of standing with her feet at an angle. "That way, the others know about us. Like the other girls. They'll know. Okay?"

For the rest of the tour, Dorothea spent the nights with me. I had not yet had a girlfriend in my life, certainly not one who was in my bed every night, but here I was with an independent Dorothea, liberated by the war, thumbing her nose at traditional inhibitions.

The tour traversed the length and breadth of Texas and Oklahoma: towns like Electra, Vernon, Odessa, Amarillo, Austin, Lubbock, San Angelo, Tulsa, Oklahoma City, and Altus. In Vernon, one of the spectators shot a rattlesnake that was slithering between the seats, and in Odessa the stage was so highly waxed, the show looked like a version of the Ice Capades. In Altus, a giant scorpion scooting along the footlights met an untimely death when one of the orchestra's saxophone players smooshed him with his mute. The show received extravagant praise in the local papers, some of it too extravagant, as was this paean in the Amarillo *Globe:* "There are few laugh provokers in America that can bring down the house as Aaron Hotchner, former Broadway stage star who was in George M. Cohen's [sic] *I'd Rather Be Right.*" (I suppose this misinformation came from the fact that I had performed in the show in college, in a nonsinging role.)

In Oklahoma City, word spread through the cast that a scout for Warner Bros. Studio would be in the audience that night. It was exciting that our reputation had reached Hollywood but it was less than exciting to learn, the following day, that Lynn Ruth Baggett, our leading lady, had signed a contract with the scout and departed for Tinseltown without telling anyone. One of the chorus girls, Carly Ramey, had been prepped as her understudy so the show was able to go on that night, but I was the one who had assured Lynn's father that we would look after his young daughter and I felt personally responsible that this had happened. I could never understand the completely masked ambition that must have motivated her to leave us in the lurch like that. I suppose she was afraid we'd try to talk her into staying, that we might phone her father. During the war, in various Air Force movie houses, I saw her in a few films, small parts, but after a couple of years she disappeared from the screen.

There is an addendum to the saga of Lynn Ruth Baggett. To recount it, I will have to move forward six years to New York City, where I got my first postwar job, as a literary bounty hunter for *Cosmopolitan* magazine (this was before sex and the single girl consumed it).

My job was to contact important writers and induce them to

write for the magazine. One of the writers on my list was Dorothy Parker, who, as a result of my visits with her, consented to write a short story for the magazine. But when I checked on its progress (I was only paid my munificent three-hundred-dollar bounty if and when I handed in the author's story), Dorothy said she had been slowed down by the unexpected arrival of the wife of the movie producer Sam Spiegel. Spiegel had renamed himself S. P. Eagle because of the anti-Semitism engendered by the Nazis, and Dorothy said that Mrs. Eagle-Spiegel had shown up at her hotel-room door battered and bruised and had dramatically installed herself in one of the beds—that was four days ago and she showed no signs of stirring except to order drinks and food from room service. Unfortunately, by nature Dorothy was much too indulgent to suggest that she was being inconvenienced, but the fact was that Mrs. Eagle-Spiegel's room-service bills were a serious matter since Dorothy was broke, not having written anything for several years. She hadn't left her room for weeks for fear of being accosted by the manager in the lobby.

There was a little-girl-lost quality about Dorothy that I found endearing, an innocent pilloried by a manipulative world, and I felt an urge to rescue her, to try to get her a respite from being imprisoned in her own hotel room with the encamped Mrs. Eagle-Spiegel. However, there was little I could do but hope that the Eagle-Spiegels would reconcile and wifey would go back to Hollywood. Dorothy finally finished her short story, entitled "The Game," but when I went to the New Westin Hotel to get it and congratulate her I found her in a surprisingly somber mood. With a quick little thrust of her head toward the bedroom, she immediately communicated the problem—Mrs. Eagle-Spiegel still occupied one of the beds. Three months and, Dorothy confided, no sign of departure. I asked her whether she had discussed the future with Mrs. Eagle-Spiegel, but she said that the woman was in such an abysmal state it would be cruel to do so. Dorothy thought it might be helpful, however, for her to introduce me so that I could convey to Mrs. Eagle-Spiegel as gently as possible that she ought to be making other bed arrangements. I really didn't want to go in and face this person, but I felt so sorry about Dorothy's haplessness that I consented.

The sheet was pulled up over the inert form on the bed, face and all, as if it were a freshly deceased body. "Lynn, dear, I'd like you to meet my good friend A. E. Hotchner, called Hotch," Dorothy said brightly.

The sheet descended like a reluctant theater curtain, Lynn Eagle-Spiegel revealing herself in slow stages: first the jet-black hair, then the large black eyes, followed by the shock of the recognizable nose and mouth. The face was thinner and the skin had lost its luminosity, but she was unmistakably Lynn Ruth Baggett. She raised her head from the pillow and looked at me with clouded eyes. "Well, if it isn't Jeep," she said.

I started to reminisce about the show in an attempt to keep her attention, but her head returned to the pillow and she never said another word. Talking to her was like trying to revive a corpse with mouth-to-mouth resuscitation. After a while, Dorothy motioned me to give up and we returned to the living room to have a drink.

The way in which Dorothy finally rid herself of Lynn was rather drastic but certainly effective—she simply packed up and moved to the Hotel Volney without telling Lynn where she was going. Lynn's reaction was to take a taxi to the airport and return to Hollywood. Since existence in Los Angeles is impossible without a car, one of Lynn's friends, the actor George Tobias, lent her one of his. The first day she had it on the road, she ran over a small child and was jailed for vehicular homicide. Not long after that, she committed suicide while out on bail. All these years I have felt a residue of guilt at having induced that young, pretty girl to leave the cosmetic counter to become an actress. The stories about Sam

Spiegel's treatment of her were not pretty. How much better off she would have been in the limited but safe confines of Wichita Falls.

As the show wound its way through the Southwest, the news from the Pacific was increasingly ominous: the Japanese over-ran our troops on Bataan, inflicting tremendous casualties, and a month later Corregidor also fell, with even more terrible casualties. On the home front, *Three Dots with a Dash* was having its own problems. Captain Young had been transferred and the dour Captain Busby, who disdained actor-soldiers, had replaced him. Among the cast there was growing resentment against the privileges of the Sylva elite, who rode staff cars and received special treatment. There was also a nasty feud brewing between the compere, Jimmy Kelly, who played piano stage left, and the two jugglers, a strange, disgruntled pair who often whizzed their tenpins perilously close to Kelly's head.

As the war news and the show's problems worsened, I grew increasingly restive about my show-business existence, a far cry from my still-burning ambition to get into some kind of action. Once again it was time for divine intervention and intervene it did, this time in the form of an advisory that was circulating to the effect that applicants were being considered for the Air Force Officer Candidate School in Miami. Just as I had induced Myron Gollub and Chris Donohue to apply, I now convinced Jack Thomas that we should forgo the greasepaint for the gold bars of a lieutenant. By then our show had raised more than a quarter of a million dollars for the relief fund, a much more significant sum in those days than now, so we could depart knowing that we had helped make a contribution to the families of servicemen who had been killed in action. Captain Busby was pleased to see us go off to OCS, and he closed down the show immediately.

# Eight

Packed into dilapidated World War I vintage trains, Jack and I were among two hundred Sheppard Field GIs who were dispatched to Miami Beach in filthy cars with torn seats and rusty, squealing wheels, pulled by a coal-burning locomotive that encrusted us with layers of bituminous soot. There were no facilities for washing other than a small basin beside a single toilet at the end of each car. Wichita Falls to Waco, Beaumont, Baton Rouge, Biloxi, Mobile, Pensacola, Tallahassee, Gainesville, Ocala, Lakeland, Naples, and finally Miami.

It took us six days to get to our destination, for we were constantly nudged onto remote sidings for long hours to let priority freight trains carrying military supplies go through. There was certainly nothing priority about us. One of our many siding delays occurred in Mississippi where, on an adjacent siding, a truckload of watermelons was being loaded into a freight car by three black men. Responding to strenuous urgings from the guys in my car, they pitched a couple of watermelons through an open window. The melons split open on the floor, the pieces ravenously set upon by all of us, who had had nothing but dry rations since we left Sheppard Field. It was a jolly interlude, all of us burying our faces in the sweet, juicy hunks of ripe melon and tossing the rinds at targets alongside the tracks. The aftermath, however, was anything but jolly as swarms of flies and other insects descended upon the sticky watermelon juice where it had been smeared on the floor and seats and on our clothing. Closing the windows would invite suffocation but since we had no bug spray, in desperation we removed our shirts and flailed away at the flies, fifty GIs with their shirts whirling around them like a band of perspiring Turkish dancers.

Our bedraggled, unwashed, soot-ridden contingent arrived in Miami Beach on the hottest June day ever recorded (in fact, as it turned out, it was to be the hottest summer ever recorded). At the end of the interminable nightmare journey from Sheppard Field I had eagerly anticipated the Miami Beach I had seen shimmering in the resort section of the *St. Louis Post-Dispatch*, but what I found was a ghost city stripped of its luxuries and vacationers. The hotels where we officer candidates were quartered had surrendered their furniture and their king-size beds, their ornate dining rooms, their rococo bars. In their places were army cots, bare rooms, and mess halls. The city was a sauna that had fractured the thermometers. There was no air-conditioning, the pools were empty, the restaurants closed, elevators nonfunctional, the beaches deserted. Nine and a half miles of luxury hotels along the beach had been turned into a military installation.

I was assigned to company Q, quartered in the Plymouth Hotel. We were issued khaki uniforms with a round OCS insignia on the breast pocket for Officer Candidate School.

The second day after our arrival, Lieutenant Murray, who commanded our squadron, sent for me. When I entered his office (formerly the Plymouth's bar, called the Rock Room—Plymouth Rock, get it?) and found him inspecting my classification card, my heart plummeted into my GI socks. Oh, no, not again!

"I see here, cadet, that you wrote a musical comedy at Sheppard Field, that right?"

I was too numb to answer.

"That right?" he repeated sternly.

"Yes, sir," I answered, not sternly. "But, please, sir . . ."

"Cadets speak when spoken to," he reminded me.

"Yes, sir."

"We need a squadron song to march to." My heart rose from my socks. "By tomorrow morning."

"A marching song?"

"Something with cadence the cadets can sing out as they march along the streets. The squadrons all compete, so give us a good rouser."

"Yes, sir."

"That's all, cadet."

"Yes, sir."

I had never written music—in fact, I didn't play an instrument—but I had written lyrics and my memory rustled up an old chestnut from a Sigmund Romberg operetta to which I put words that I hoped would fill the bill. Write corny, I told myself, don't try to be creative. No fancy rhymes. Hut hoot heet four.

Marching along together
We're the men of squadron Q
No matter what the weather
We're the men of derring-do!

And so forth.

All that summer the cadets of squadron Q marched along the streets of Miami Beach, shouting the song with uninhibited gusto. Lieutenant Murray said it was "a right good tune." I didn't mention Romberg because I hadn't been asked and a cadet never spoke unless spoken to.

Cadet: the very sound of the word was a surge of military promise; cadet, a West Point resonance; cadet, ramrod straight, chin in, squared-off salute, purposeful stride. Cadet, a somebody, not a GI glob on the Sheppard Field drill field. Cadet, the cocoon from which a second lieutenant would emerge, *if*—and it was a big if—the candidate could survive the inhuman obstacles placed in his path: difficult daily classroom assignments, obstacle courses with soaring walls to climb over and low-slung barbed wire to wriggle under, demanding drill field maneuvers, full-pack hikes over challenging terrain, dusty firing ranges (top scores required), night patrols, penalty calisthenics.

Every day at four o'clock, the hottest part of the blistering day, we had to march with rifles on the parade ground where the temperature was easily 130 degrees, often being required to stand motionless in ranks for extended periods of time. If a man fainted once, he got a demerit; twice, he was washed out. As we stood erect with our chins on our chests, the sweat pouring into our eyes, we could hear the sound of the ambulances, called meat wagons, as they skirted the rear files, picking up cadets who had passed out. If one of the cadets fainted during the parade march, we were required to keep stride, even if it meant stepping on him, and sometimes an entire company would tramp over an unconscious body. Thirteen weeks of the most grueling mental and physical hell imaginable, on the theory that if you could get through these eighteen-hour days you could survive anything the war might throw at you. We were kept in a constant state of nervous and physical exhaustion, the purpose being to crack us if they possibly could and wash us out as potential officers.

Also quartered at Miami Beach was the Officers Training School, which was looked upon with scorn by those of us in OCS, for these were the dentists, lawyers, Hollywood big shots, doctors, politicians, et cetera, who were given direct commissions and stayed in a posh section of Miami only long enough to get outfitted in their custom-made uniforms and given a few lectures in a country-club atmosphere. The big story of that summer was that Clark Gable had been offered one of these cushy OTS commissions but had turned it down in favor of going through the thirteen weeks of OCS like an ordinary GI. His induction had been widely publicized, and besieging mobs along the route of the train that brought him from Hollywood had delayed his arrival in Miami.

I had entered OCS a few weeks before Gable, and I saw him from afar on the day he arrived as he strode down the street on his way to his assigned hotel, a handsome, erect figure moving purposefully as a phalanx of reporters strove to keep up with him. I didn't see him again until late one afternoon, after the daily parade, when on my way back to the Plymouth Hotel I came upon a rumpled, sweaty cadet seated on a bench at a bus stop with the shoe and stocking removed from his left foot. "You wouldn't have a pin on you, would you?" he asked.

It was Gable, but I recognized the voice more than the man himself; his famous mustache was gone (OCS regulation), he had a semi–crew cut (also a regulation), his khaki shirt was soaked through, and there were blisters on his foot the size of half-dollars. I was surprised to see vestiges of gray in his hair. There was an angry-looking pimple on his nose. He looked wilted and old to my young eyes, and I was amazed to think how much younger he had looked a couple of years before in *Gone with the Wind*. He was forty-one, almost twice my age, and it was obvious that the ordeal of trying to keep up with kids in their twenties was taking its toll on him.

I always kept a needle pinned inside my belt loop for my own blisters, but after looking at his foot I suggested he go to the infirmary and get proper treatment.

"Well," he said, "I'd like to, but there would be such flak over my coming down with a few blisters . . ."

I understood. If you're Clark Gable you are not allowed to get blisters; the heroic seaman of *Mutiny on the Bounty* would not get blisters. I punctured the blisters with my needle and gushes of liquid ran down his foot and dripped onto the bus bench. There must have been a dozen blisters.

Afterward we went to the canteen and had a Coke (we were allowed one hour of free time each day after the parade). Looking as he did, bereft of his mustache, his crew cut giving prominence to his wide ears, his uniform sagging with perspiration, he didn't get any attention from the cadets in the canteen. It was suffocatingly hot. Gable said he was having a tough time. "I didn't realize I was such an old fart until I got here with you kids," he said. "I thought I was in pretty good shape . . ."

I assured him he'd tough it out.

"I may not. That hike today, my backpack felt like four hundred pounds. My legs were gone. They woke us up at three o'clock in the morning and gave us two minutes to fall out in the street in full uniform. I forgot my goddamn garters and got two demerits. I'll have to march an hour of penalty on Saturday. Why the shit do they make us wear garters?"

"So they can give us demerits."

"The heat's really getting to me—and I've got a long time to go. I really don't know if I'll make it."

"Sure you will—you're the last person they would flunk out."

"Yeah, well, maybe they will—just to demonstrate that OCS is so tough and impartial they can even flunk Clark Gable."

I had to admit that was a possibility.

I saw Gable once more, two weeks later, at a mustering for nighttime guard duty on the beach. We were patrolling the beaches because on the night of June 16, the very day I arrived at OCS, German submarine U-584 had approached the Florida coast, switched its motors from diesel to electric to mute the sound, and maneuvered within fifty yards of the shore at Ponte Vedra, a short distance north of Miami. A rubber dinghy was inflated and boarded by four passengers, Nazi agents highly trained in military and industrial sabotage. They placed four black wooden cases, two feet long by a foot wide, a shovel, and four small canvas bags in the dinghy, which reached shore in a matter of minutes. The saboteurs and their possessions were deposited on the beach and the dinghy swiftly returned to the U-boat, which immediately departed.

The saboteurs dug holes at the base of nearby palm trees and buried the boxes. The shovel was thrown into the ocean. The men then opened their canvas bags and removed American clothing, which they changed into. That done, they walked to a nearby filling station where they knew they could catch a bus for Jacksonville. German intelligence had prepared them very well. The four of them checked into Jacksonville hotels and enjoyed a good dinner, paying for it from the thousands of dollars in their money belts.

Synchronized with the 584's landing at Ponte Vedra, U-boat 202 was at the same time disgorging four similar saboteurs on the Long Island shore at Amagansett. These men were equipped with identical black boxes, which they also buried, and canvas bags with American clothing.

With the contents of those black boxes, these eight men would be able to wreak havoc on domestic shipping and manufacture. Scientists in a laboratory in Germany masterminded by the Abwehr, the intelligence corps devoted to sabotage, had invented ingenious devices that were the prototypes for gimmicks that were used, years later, in the James Bond movies. Six of the eight boxes contained bricks that were hollow and filled with the Abwehr's especially destructive dynamite, and bombs made to look like lumps of coal. The two remaining boxes contained timing devices, safety and detonating fuses, pen-and-pencil sets that were incendiaries filled with sulfuric acid, rounds of wire, and a variety of other destructive devices. All eight saboteurs, who spoke English, had once lived in the United States and had returned to Germany when Hitler began his conquest of Europe.

The entire operation, code-named Pastorius, was headed by a Nazi named Walter Kappe who, until 1939, had been an officer of

Camp Siegfried, run by the German-American Bund at Yaphank, Long Island. Three of the four men who landed in Florida had also belonged to that camp, which glorified Hitler and celebrated his conquests. On Sundays, forty thousand American Bundists would gather at the camp, wearing the martial uniform of the Bund—black breeches and boots, gray shirts, and black ties. They would parade carrying flags emblazoned with swastikas, exchange stiff-armed salutes, and sing the Nazi anthem, "The Horst Wessel Song": "When Jewish blood drips from the knife, Then will the German people prosper."

Kappe gave violent anti-Semitic lectures and headed a committee that plotted espionage and sabotage efforts. He promised that Siegfrieders would become the storm troopers of America. A large portrait of Hitler hung on the wall of the camp's restaurant and considerable sums of money were raised for Nazi causes in Germany. Camp streets were named after Nazi heroes—Himmler Street, Göring Street, and so forth. Before the camp was disbanded by government action, Kappe had been ordered to return to Germany to organize Operation Pastorius.

Although they were still at large when we began our beach patrol, it would later be discovered that the Florida contingent made its way to New York City, where they registered at the Commodore Hotel, while the Long Island men traveled to Chicago. The two groups planned to rendezvous in Cincinnati on July 4, at which time they would organize their sabotage of communication lines, basic industries, airports, and railroads. Specifically targeted was the Chesapeake & Ohio Railroad, one of the nation's primary coal transporters. By sabotaging bridges, tunnels, and key terminals on the C&O's lines, production would be impaired at steel mills and other plants that depended on coal mined in West Virginia and Pennsylvania. Other key targets were the factories of the Aluminum Company of America at Alcoa, Tennessee; Massena, New York; and East St. Louis. An associated target was the Philadelphia Salt Company's cryolite plant, which produced material vital to aluminum production.

When I was assigned to night patrol, we didn't know any of this, only that eight Nazis were on the loose and we were on four-hour patrol shifts, from dusk to dawn, to guard against the landing of any more saboteurs. Gable was in the group I was assigned to, and we wound up paired for the midnight to 4 A.M. shift on one of the beaches. The password for the night was "American Eagle." We were instructed to shoot anyone who appeared on the beach and didn't know those magic words. Our weapon was a heavy, clumsy gun that had been used in World War I. All the modern Garands were being supplied to combat forces overseas, and the antiquated Enfield was the best that ordnance could do. (We also had to lug them around the parade grounds in that beastly heat.) It was a backbreaking four hours, patrolling the desolate beach with our heavy boots sinking into the wet sand, the Enfields weighing a ton on our shoulders, the night air equatorially hot and steamy. The moon glinted innocently over the placid water.

"You got your needle?" Gable asked.

"Always at the ready."

"My feet feel like I'm going to need it. Can you imagine having to shoot this gun and hit anything? I hope one of those OTS dentists comes along—I'd like to test it."

Each time we reached the perimeter of our area, we put down our rifles and took a short break before turning around and retracing our steps. After a couple of hours of this monotony, Gable dropped his rifle and plunked himself down on the sand.

"Pa's gotta rest his weary dogs."

I plopped down on the beach beside him.

"That's what she used to call me—Pa, and I called her Ma," he said softly. He started to smoke a cigarette, carefully cupping his hand around the glowing end. He started to talk about his wife, Carole Lombard, the movie actress who had recently died in a as he swam out to the buoy. Jack gave me a look. "I'll be a son of a bitch," he said, "you can't swim, can you?"

When our turn came, as we waded through the surf to the deeper water, I subtly took hold of the back of Jack's swim pants and held on for dear life as he started to swim toward the buoy, all the while making swimming motions with my right arm. Halfway to the buoy, he stopped and, treading water, said, "You're on your own now, kid. I'll keep an eye on you." Whereupon he pushed my hand off him and took off. After a moment of splashing panic, I realized, to my amazement, that although my feet were not touching the distant bottom, I was not drowning. Somehow, using a splashing technique new to natation, I propelled myself to the buoy and back to the beach. The officer who was administering the test looked at me quizzically as I staggered out of the surf and gave his head a sad waggle, but he did check me off on the swim column.

If I had won a gold medal in the Olympic games or hit a home in to win the World Series or been awarded a Nobel Prize, none them could have compared to the burst of pride I felt on the rnoon we graduated. Wearing my new officer's uniform with bars on my shoulders and Air Force insignia on the lapels, eived my OCS certificate, smartly saluted the commanding , and became a second lieutenant. I also felt a great sense of ecause in view of my track record for last-minute derail- I fully expected another one. But now I had triumphed flat feet, my non-depth perception, and the musical- monkey on my back.

me afternoon we received our assignments and, from of it, I was about to embark on the military mission I d about: Lieutenant Hotchner, Adjutant of the 13th rine Wing of the United States Air Force, Westover ee Falls, Massachusetts. I was informed that the 13th

plane crash while on a tour to sell war bonds. He said that for the past hour, as we silently tramped the beach, he had been reliving wonderful times with her. He told me about their first duck shoot, early in the morning, the fog too thick to see the ducks, although you could hear them. Carole asked what they could do about it. Just sit here in the blind until it clears, Clark told her. She said she had just thought of something they could do while they were waiting. "We made love," Clark said, "which ain't easy in a duck blind."

He made a funny little sound; I thought he was chortling over the incident, but in the moonlight I could see his tears. He continued to weep as he told me about the evening that Carole, dressed in a smashing white evening gown, jumped into a fishpond, and he told me about the dogs they had given each other, the silly picnics Carole arranged, the Sundays alone on their ranch, and their ludicrous attempt to go into the egg business, all the while making little observations about films and Hollywood life that I didn't really understand, but what I did understand was the enormous love Gable had had for this woman. In a sense, it was unreal that Clark Gable was sitting there with me on the wet sand weeping over the loss of his movie-star wife, but the pressures of OCS had pushed him close to the edge.

"They think I don't know," he said, "but I do—what they found of her—I know . . . decapitated, and the rest of her burned to nothing." He fished inside his shirt and brought out two chains, one that held his dog tag, the other a small locket that he opened. It contained a fragment of jeweled metal. He said that that was the only thing of hers that hadn't burned—the fragment was from a diamond-and-ruby clip he had given to her.

He put the memento away and we were just getting up to resume our patrol when a piercing shot exploded in the night, followed by shouts and a form running pell-mell along the sidewalk at the crest of the beach. We learned that Gable's wish had been fulfilled—some OTS instant captain who didn't know the pass-word had gone for a stroll and had run afoul of the sentry on the adjoining beach, who had fired at him but missed.

Gable got a good laugh out of that, and for the rest of our tour he talked about various hunting and fishing trips, but didn't mention Carole Lombard again.

That was the last time I saw him. But he did succeed in graduating from OCS and eventually flew a series of combat missions.

Within a month after they entered the United States, and before they could initiate any of their nefarious projects, all eight of the saboteurs had been captured by the FBI and put behind bars as a result of a bizarre defection by one of their group who thought he would gain immunity and a reward if he went to the FBI and gave them the whereabouts of his fellow saboteurs. But the military commission that tried these men sentenced all of them to death by electrocution, although they recommended that the sentences of two of them be commuted to life imprisonment because of their assistance in the apprehension and conviction of the others.

In compliance, President Roosevelt commuted one sentence to life at hard labor and the other to thirty years at hard labor. The remaining six men were electrocuted on August 8, 1942. In 1948, after serving five years of their sentences, by order of President Harry Truman the two men in prison were deported to Germany.

The OCS classroom work was demanding but in itself not impossibly difficult; coupled with my mental and physical exhaustion, however, it was like being quizzed on Einstein's theory of relativity. Some groggy cadets simply couldn't focus on the classroom work and when they came up short on the frequent exams, they were unceremoniously shipped out to some infelicitous reassignment center. For me, however, the biggest hurdle I had to overcome was not the classroom or the obstacle course or the

firing range but the beach. Every cadet was required to demonstrate that he could swim, a prerequisite that worried me from day one. In St. Louis the only places one could swim were the muddy Mississippi River, which featured catfish, leeches, and assorted flotsam, and the murky, overcrowded pool at the Highland amusement park, which charged an exorbitant two-dollar admission fee for splashing space, if you could manage to find any. I had previously been faced with the same swimming crisis when I was a teenaged counselor at Camp Hawthorne in the Ozarks, but by cleverly scheduling alternate activities during the swimming periods I was able to avoid drowning myself in view of my campers. It was not as if I had not tried and hard to get myself afloat. During those two summers at the in the evening when the waterfront was deserted I wo down to the swimming crib that was set in the lake a ately try to induce my feet to lift off the bottom. up and down, dip my head, get one foot up, tr swallow several mouthfuls of lake water, and cho the crib's wooden side slat. On one occasion, w casin dropped off an overhanging branch in six campers immediately jumped overboar with the choice of diving into the water o deadly snake, I stayed put and attacked t with a paddle, luckily smashing him b into me.

But there was no way I could av day squadron Q was scheduled consisted of groups of eight cad While my group waited its tu that had a glimmer of possi took Jack Thomas aside a pull going over the obsta I hold on to the side o

Wing hunted German U-boats with B-24s and B-25s equipped with depth charges, and I would be the administrative officer in charge of B-25 operations. My orders were expedited because the wing was on alert to embark for an air base in North Africa, to patrol the U-boat-infested waters of the Strait of Gibraltar. I was now a commissioned officer on a serious combat mission, and I was certain nothing could deter me this time.

I was dead wrong.

# Nine

My travel orders to Westover Field contained a three-day rest and recreation stopover in New York City, providing me with a welcome respite after the grueling three months of OCS at steamy Miami Beach. The quartermaster assigned me a room at the Henry Hudson Hotel, which had been requisitioned by the Air Force for transient personnel. I was given a per diem of seven dollars, which might have been enough to cover expenses in some places but not New York City. As it turned out, however, I was virtually subsidized by New Yorkers everywhere I went.

There was a patriotic spirit in the city that came as a surprise because from all I had read I expected New Yorkers to be aggressive and indifferent. Instead, everywhere I went—restaurants, bars, hotel lobbies, the subway, walking along the sidewalks—people couldn't have been friendlier and seemed as proud of my uniform as I was. In restaurants, the waiters often informed me that my check had been taken care of by patriotic diners; in bars, drinks were often on the house; the officers' lounge at the Commodore Hotel had free tickets for Broadway plays and concerts. In fact, the Commodore lounge was staffed with young, attractive volunteers from some of New York's tonier women's clubs. The lounge had a policy of not allowing dates with the officers, but the young women were pleasant companions for those of us who frequented the place. I will always remember a lovely young volunteer named Harriet who insisted that I try my first clam. She was in charge of a sideboard filled with attractive seafood, and on hearing that I had never eaten a clam (in landlocked St. Louis, shellfish was an expensive rarity of dubious freshness), she insisted that I try one.

It took courage, but I met the challenge. And subsequently, at her insistence, I conquered my first oyster.

As I said, there was a spirit in the city, a camaraderie, a sense of purpose, a common bond, that was unique to that time; in all the years I have lived in New York as a civilian, that spirit was never duplicated (until the period that followed the September 11 debacle in 2001). There were rather severe rations, regulated by ration books that contained coupons for such necessities as gasoline (three gallons a week), sugar, meat, and shoes, to name a few, but most everyone accepted these deprivations as patriotic necessities.

The rooms at the Henry Hudson were small and spare, but the luxury of having a room to myself after months of communal living was wonderfully welcome. On my second night there, I was annoyed by a loud radio coming at me from the adjoining room. I went out in the hall and knocked on the door, intending to request the officer to give me a break on the volume, but I was startled when my neighbor turned out to be an attractive young woman in a WAC officer's uniform. She invited me in to share the music, her bottle of Wild Turkey, and peanut-butter crackers. Before the night ended, Dottie and I also shared her narrow bed. In the uncertain atmosphere of the war, time was measured in quick intervals that momentarily grounded the uncertainty. Dottie was headed to the Pacific theater of war and I was destined for Africa to hunt submarines, so shared nights were not likely to come our way for a long time to come. The liberation of women began back then, long before NOW and the wave of the sixties. A year after that night at the Henry Hudson, I received a long-delayed letter from Dottie informing me that she had risen in rank to first lieutenant, and her APO number indicated that she was somewhere in the South Pacific. I never heard from her again.

# TEN

Westover Field was located adjacent to the Massachusetts town of Chicopee Falls, a short distance north of Springfield. This part of Massachusetts had once been a prosperous manufacturing center, turning out half of the nation's shoes and cotton products and a third of its woolen goods, but labor strife that involved bloody strikes and sit-ins, plus the paralyzing effects of the Depression, had shut down many of its factories and the rest lost business to factories in the South that could produce their products more cheaply by using nonunion, low-paid workers.

Westover Field had been hurriedly built in 1940 as the German army began to overrun one European country after another. Fourteen hundred workers of the Civilian Conservation Corps and Works Projects Administration had been sent to Chicopee to clear tobacco and farm fields. When Hitler's troops smashed into Holland, Belgium, Luxembourg, and France at dawn on May 10, 1940, the pace of construction had begun to accelerate and on those cleared tobacco fields huge steel and brick hangars had been constructed. Airfields were springing up all over the country and aircraft production was also greatly accelerated. When France fell in June of 1940, military aircraft production in the United States was only four hundred planes a month, but by the end of the following year it was twenty-five hundred a month and increasing. Westover was a hub for assembling P-40 fighters, the planes arriving on flatbed railroad cars with the fuselage in one box and the wings and propellers in another. As soon as they were assembled, inspected, and tested, they were flown directly into combat zones. Crews of these planes were also assembled and trained at Westover, which, in early 1942, switched its activities to anti-submarine warfare. Most of the squadrons of the 13th Wing flew B-24s, slow aircraft that were better suited for patrolling the water than the B-25s that were the aircraft of my squadron.

The B-25 had distinctive twin fins and was powered by a pair of 1700 hp engines that gave it a top speed of 272 mph and a range of 1,350 miles with a full load of six 500-pound bombs. It carried a crew of six, consisting of bombardier/gunner, pilot, copilot, top turret gunner, tail gunner, and waist gunner. The bombardier was stationed in the translucent nose of the plane, where he had a commanding view of the forward area.

For me, the allure of being stationed in Massachusetts was the fact that so many of my literary heroes had come from there or had lived there—Hawthorne, Longfellow, Emerson, Thoreau, Melville, and a host of others. Massachusetts also seemed to spawn an inordinate number of savants, politicians, and scientists, and many of the glamour universities that I had been in awe of were located there.

But Westover Field had nothing in common with any of those aspects of life in Massachusetts. Westover was an enclave with rigid security and a total commitment to hunting down German submarines. At this time, September 1942, large numbers of diesel-electric U-boats were terrorizing British and American ships in the Atlantic. Most of these were 500- to 700-ton U-boats supplemented by 1,000- to 1,600-ton U-cruisers. The cruisers were needed for long-range operations and to refuel smaller submarines at sea. The Germans kept the smaller U-boats prowling the sea-lanes in wolf packs. In the first six months of 1943, they sank approximately seven hundred merchant ships and were boldly operating very close to the eastern seaboard of the United States. The submarines that had landed the spies on the Florida beach when I was at OCS had been released from a U-cruiser.

⊬ By the time I arrived at Westover Field, the Air Force was just beginning to limit the U-boats' effectiveness by incessantly bombing submarine bases in Germany and by patrolling the waters with depth charges. They were also convoying U.S. ships with long-range bombers. Later in the war, submarine mines, sonar, torpedo nets, and noisemakers helped end the submarine menace. Particularly effective was the noisemaker, which was towed behind a ship and drew acoustically guided torpedoes away from the hull.

I learned about the German subs in briefings that were held for all new arrivals, a group that was primarily made up of flight crews, pilots, and bombardiers who were joining the 13th Wing to increase the number of planes on submarine surveillance. My squadron flew B-25s, medium attack bombers that were much too fast for the type of methodical reconnaissance that was most effective, but the B-25 was the predominant aircraft available, a glamour plane that had been produced in quantity after it was flown by Lieutenant Colonel James Doolittle and his group in their celebrated raid on the Japanese homeland.

Shortly after Pearl Harbor, when the nation was shocked and jittery over its catastrophic losses, Colonel Doolittle had proposed an air attack on Tokyo as a morale booster to counter the Pearl Harbor fiasco. Although his superior officers were skeptical, Doolittle was given permission to attempt what seemed to be a foolhardy venture. With sixteen volunteer Air Force crews, he secretly prepared for the special mission, flying B-25s. On the morning of April 18, 1942, four months after Pearl Harbor, Doolittle and his group of B-25s took off from the aircraft carrier *Hornet* and wave-hopped five hundred miles toward Japan, flying at treetop level over the mainland. They encountered no opposition and were able to drop their bombs on Yokohama, Kobe, Nagoya, and Tokyo, then head for prearranged airfields in eastern China.

Doolittle's raid had little military effect but, as he had intended, it had an enormous impact on both Japanese and American morale. Having been assured that their country was invulnerable to attack, the Japanese were shocked by the bold raid. Americans, on the other hand, saw it as a show of retribution for Pearl Harbor. Doolittle's thirty seconds over Tokyo was the first positive action since the war began and it was a shot in the arm for the whole country. Everywhere I went people talked about it, exaggerating our accomplishments because it was the only bright spot among the dark, forbidding bulletins that appeared in the newspapers day after day like an epidemic of obituaries. One after the other, the Japanese invaded Burma, Borneo, Hong Kong, Manila, the Netherlands Indies, Rabaul, the Solomons, Singapore, Bali, and New Guinea, and on April 9, 1942, our forces on Bataan surrendered to the Japanese after a ninety-eight-day siege, the cruelest blow of all. Nine days after Bataan fell, Doolittle's B-25s dropped their bombs.

But we paid a price for the raid. Bad weather and strong headwinds kept the aircraft from their target fields in China. All sixteen of the planes were lost. The crews of eleven planes bailed out, four planes crash-landed, and one was able to reach Vladivostok in Russia, where both the B-25 and the crew were interned. Seven crew members were injured, three were killed, and eight were taken prisoner by the Japanese, who executed them. The other survivors, who had landed in territory controlled by the Japanese, were rescued by sympathetic Chinese, who hid them in their villages. The Japanese occupying forces in China inflicted severe punishment on these villages but they did not betray the American airmen.

Two days after I joined the outfit, I was scheduled to familiarize myself with its surveillance techniques by flying a four-hour mission in one of our search planes. This would be my first time in any kind of airplane, and it turned out to be a disastrous introduction to flying. The B-25 was a high-speed, highly maneuverable plane, designed to change position and altitude quickly to evade enemy fire in order to search the areas contained in the quadrants of the surveillance grid. It had to make several passes over each area, turning at abrupt angles, swooping down to investigate anything suspicious on the surface, and then pulling up abruptly to resume search at a higher altitude. Every surface boat had to be buzzed to be sure that it was not a supply tender for the U-boats. Every line of disturbed water was swooped down upon to be sure it was not a sub's snorkel, which was a long tube projecting just above the surface to provide the U-boat with air while it was submerged. During my flight, every such moving line that we swooped down on and circled turned out to be a school of dolphins or other large fish.

The depth charges we carried were not traditional bombs but cylindrical drums, like oil drums, which were loaded with explosives that would detonate at a certain depth or on contact with a submarine. The bombardier was situated in the nose of the plane and, on sighting a sub, his job was to alert the pilot, who would fly low over the suspected spot as the bombardier released the cylinders from the bomb bay.

My position in the narrow cockpit was on a cramped seat in back of the copilot. On takeoff, there was heavy vibration from the two powerful engines that thrust the plane into a quickly escalating ascent, allowing us to lift off with a minimum of run, which explained how the B-25s were able to take off from the *Hornet* for the Tokyo attack. But this quick, powerful, takeoff had a downside, and that was my stomach. I get queasy in elevators, and after fifteen minutes of patrol my stomach served notice that it was about to do its own takeoff. I emitted telltale sounds, trying to subdue my escalating gorge, but I was fast losing the battle when the copilot, a snotty fellow who wore two gold rings, a gold-link bracelet, and a gold wristwatch, reached behind his seat and handed me an empty, lidless Maxwell House Coffee can. He also slid the window open next to my head; obviously, I wasn't the first neophyte who needed Maxwell's hospitality. For those interminable hours, diving to observe fishing boats and other objects on the ocean's surface (none of which turned out to have any connection with the enemy), I made deposit after deposit into the can with contents Mr. Maxwell never envisioned for his product, and repeatedly emptied it out the window. It was a truly embarrassing, sickening performance on my first wartime mission.

As I had been informed by the assignment officer at OCS, my squadron was indeed on alert for departure to North Africa but we were not yet restricted to base. Some evenings, a couple of other officers and I would go into Chicopee Falls to have a few beers at one of the local bars. Most of the old factories in the area had been converted or activated to make munitions, duffel bags, tents, shoes, uniforms, and other materials that were in seriously short supply, and the bars were crowded with new workers, mostly women, wartime girls who had replaced men at operating machinery once considered too physically demanding or dangerous or complicated for women. Most of these women were quite young and had assumed many of the characteristics of the male workers who had once performed similar jobs. The girls crowded the bars at night, where they played the jukeboxes, smoked, drank heartily, and picked up men (mostly GIs). I recall how surprised I was on my first visit to The Rusty Nail when a group of four young women sent a note to our table, hastily scribbled on the back of a paper napkin: "Hello, boys, would you like to join us?" Another sign of the changing times.

Also changing were jobs in towns like Chicopee Falls, which had lost most of its young men to the draft. Young women replaced them in jobs that had been the special prerogative of men: bus drivers, policemen and firemen, sanitation workers, street repair, construction, plumbing and electricity, mail delivery, truck drivers, operators of steam shovels and hydraulic machinery—jobs that were still reserved for men in the military but now out of necessity were allocated to women on the home front. It was indeed startling to see, for the first time, a young, attractive woman with her hair tucked up under a police cap or a fireman's helmet. The Rusty Nail had a small dance floor in front of the jukebox and I recall how taken aback I was when a pretty blonde asked me to dance, not something that ever happened in proper St. Louis, Missouri. The blonde, who said she was a manicurist from Boston, now worked in a nearby factory as a welder. "Acetylene torch and all that?" I asked. "Yeah, and all that," she said. "I weld the axles for army trucks."

As adjutant, it was my job, with the help of three enlisted men on my staff, to oversee our departure for North Africa. The week before leaving, the men in our squadron were sequestered to base and briefed by an officer who had flown from Tunisia to Westover for that purpose. We were given booster shots for malaria, yellow fever, and typhoid, and provided with special clothing, gas masks, and boots; officers were issued sidearms. I had had gun instruction at OCS and had spent hours on the firing range, but signing for my own weapon brought home to me that I was finally going to participate in military action in a theater of war.

Or so I thought.

On the Wednesday before our scheduled Saturday deployment, I was told to report to Lieutenant Colonel R. C. Brackett, the commander of the 13th Wing, whom I was meeting for the first time. My immediate commander was Major Frischel, who was in charge of my squadron. My expectation was that Colonel Brackett wanted to check on our readiness, and I reported with all my paperwork.

But when the attaché ushered me into the colonel's office, I was faced with an ominous sight: Colonel Brackett was leaning back in his chair, looking at my eight-by-ten classification card. My first panicked reaction was that I had somehow screwed up and was being transferred to some miserable outpost.

"Have a seat, Lieutenant," Colonel Brackett said pleasantly enough. "We've got something to talk over." He turned over my classification card and pointed to an entry. "Says here you did a theater piece for Sheppard Field—looks like you toured all over the place . . ."

Oh, no, God help me. Not another musical! My stomach fell worse than in the B-25.

"You are just the man for the job."

Oh, no, you don't—I'll be court-martialed before I do another goddamn musical.

"Now this is the deal," the colonel said, tossing my card on his desk. "The 13th Wing's doing one hell of a job on those fucking U-boats, but we ain't getting credit for it. Air Force operations, but Navy gets all the credit. Christ, our wing's spotted more subs last six months, more oil slicks from depth charges, more shit on the surface, than all the Navy searchers lumped together. But we're a secret, see? Goddamn phantom outfit because no one in the high brass knows that we're doing as good at sea as we are bombing their sub bases in Bremen. A light hid under a bushel, where General Hap Arnold can't see it. Now, this is where you come in, to put the light on us, Lieutenant."

For the life of me, I couldn't see how a musical comedy was going to shine a light on the anti-submarine command. "Colonel, sir, I don't think a musical comedy would be an appropriate vehicle for achieving . . ."

"Who said anything about a musical comedy, Lieutenant?" he growled as he came forward in his chair and thrust his chin at me. "That's not your mission. What you're gonna do is make a movie that's gonna put us on the map, show off what we do, me briefing the men, the ordnance, the training, the planes in flight, dropping their charges, bombing the shit out of the fucking U-boats, music playing good and loud, know what I mean? You seen enough of those fake Hollywood turds, now we give 'em the real thing. Make myself clear?"

I had a little trouble disengaging my tongue. "Sir, Colonel, sir, I think there's some . . . some mistake here. I know absolutely, positively nothing about moviemaking. Or cameras. I just don't do photography. I'm sure there's someone in the outfit . . ."

His chin came at me again. "Lieutenant, what did they teach you at OCS?" Pause while his eyes burned two holes in my forehead. "To be *resilient,* right? Whatever happens—you get captured, whatever—you figure a way out, right? So you need to make a movie, you make a goddamn movie. You can make a musical comedy, you can make a movie."

"But, sir, does it really matter who gets the credit—the Navy or us—as long as we get the job done?"

"Does it matter? *Does it matter?*" Bulging veins appeared above his squinting eyes. "What's that patch on your shoulder? What's on your tunic? The Air Force wings, right? Are you proud to be wearing them?"

"Oh, yes, sir, very proud."

"Then, goddammit, that's why we need this movie. Case closed."

"But, Colonel, sir"—I was grasping at disappearing straws now—"my squadron is leaving for Africa Saturday and I'm the adjutant."

"Lieutenant, who am I?"

"Who are . . . why, sir, you're Lieutenant Colonel Brackett."

"Excellent. Now what do I do around here?"

"Why, you're the commander of the wing."

"Excellent. Now does it occur to you that the commander of the wing knows every adjutant in every squadron and maybe knows which squadrons are going where since he's the one sending them there?"

"I'm sorry, sir, it was presumptuous . . ."

"The adjutant of the 22nd Squadron will take over for you. Give him your files. I'll get you some space at our installation at 90 Church Street in New York. I need your movie by the end of next month so we can release it before the July budget allotment at the Pentagon. Clear?"

If I were blindfolded in front of a firing squad I could not have felt worse. "Yes, sir," I croaked out of my constricted throat. "Will I have any assistance?"

"My personnel officer is searching the roster."

"How do I get all the equipment and . . ."

"Lieutenant, what did we just discuss?"

"Resilience, sir, you mentioned resilience."

"You got it. General Larson has been brigadier for a long time— he wants another star, so make the general a helluva jazz-ass movie, hey?"

I stumbled to my feet, saluted, and Second Lieutenant Hotchner, formerly a combat adjutant, now went off on the perilous mission of making a jazz-ass movie, God help him.

# Eleven

Ninety Church Street turned out to be a Wall Street skyscraper that had been commandeered by a huge bureaucracy of Navy officers; a small section of offices had been allotted to Air Force units, and in one of those units I was assigned a couple of rooms for my movie venture. There was a gray metal desk and chair in one room and a table peppered with coffee-cup rings in the other. Metal venetian blinds were on the windows. There was a picture of General Hap Arnold, the commander of the Air Force, in back of the desk, and a portrait of FDR on the wall above the table. Other than that, the offices were bare and the walls needed paint. I requisitioned a typewriter and set myself up at the metal desk, where I proceeded to write a scenario and a commentary for the movie as best I could.

The staff that Colonel Brackett sent me consisted of two enlisted men recruited from among the ground crew at Westover Field: Sergeant David Walker and Sergeant Will Brown. Before the war, Walker, a cheerful, voluble fellow, took wedding photographs in his hometown of Buford, Georgia, and Brown, glum and mute, had previously worked in the darkroom for a photographer in Ridgewood, Ohio, developing and enlarging film. Neither had ever had a movie camera in his hands or knew anything about moviemaking, and, to make matters worse, they were intimidated by New York's hustle and bustle and resentful at being stationed in Lieutenant Hotchner's Church Street operation—but no more unhappy than the lieutenant himself, who yearned to be in North Africa with a sidearm on his hip.

The peculiar thing about my Air Force orders was that although I had been directed to establish a headquarters and produce a film, there was no provision for a superior officer to whom I would be accountable, which meant that I could run my operation any way I chose. My first priority was to get the equipment I needed to get started, but the problem with that was that I had no idea what equipment I needed. I found out that Twentieth-Century Fox had offices on the far West Side of Manhattan, and although I didn't know who to ask for, the receptionist arranged for me to see one of the executives, who helped me compose a detailed shopping list of items I had never heard of before. I sent the list, marked "Urgent," to the Air Force supply depot in Dayton, Ohio, and within days an overwhelming supply of material began arriving—office furniture, hundreds of reels of film, two large refrigerators in which to keep the film, a photostat machine the size of a tank, projectors, screens, Bell & Howell cameras, viewfinders, Moviolas and other editing equipment, an array of chemicals, camera tracks, lifts, hoists, and hundreds of items I had checked off, with the help of my Twentieth-Century Fox contact, in the Dayton inventory of motion-picture equipment available. Unfortunately, it was not possible to order a modest quantity of anything since the supply depot was geared to large-unit shipments and most of what I requested came in prepacked crates and boxes. Much of the technical equipment—such as Eymo cameras, sound booms connected to intricate control panels, and scores of sophisticated lenses that required special operators—were stored away and never used.

My overall philosophy as the mastermind of this operation was to shoot as much footage as possible and pray that out of every thousand feet we filmed, ten feet might be usable. After many trial runs, we began to film at Westover Field, using 16mm Bell & Howell hand-operated cameras. These cameras had no batteries or electrical access and had to be wound like a clock. They could run for thirty seconds or so before they ran down and had to be rewound. As a result, the movie had to be restricted to rather short takes.

The more footage we shot, the bolder I became. I arranged for special B-25 search runs that I could film (my stomach was tentatively accepting the dives, rolls, swerves, and circles) with Sergeant Walker pointing his camera from the bombardier's position in the transparent nose, backed up by Sergeant Brown, who kept a wound camera at the ready. I really exercised my power as the Cecil B. DeMille of the Air Force on the day I arranged with the commanding officer of the submarine base in Norfolk for the U.S. submarine *Tuna* to be sent on special assignment to the Atlantic waters off the Massachusetts coast; at the same time I arranged for a B-25 and its crew to be assigned to me so that we could film reconnaissance runs with the B-25 dropping its depth charges (dummies) on the *Tuna*, thereby demonstrating the technique used on an anti-submarine mission.

As filming progressed, I became more audacious in my use of the camera. On one occasion, to get the proper taxiing and take-off shots, I borrowed an enormous derrick from an engineer battalion and, by means of ropes and pulleys, I hoisted Walker and Brown to its top. They had become quite adept at filming by now, having learned to use a variety of lenses in the process. Employing a hit-or-miss method, I was gradually able to assemble some footage that looked halfway decent.

We shot twenty times more stuff than I could possibly use. But despite the miles of footage I accumulated and stored in the refrigerators, I did not have a climax, footage of our bombers in a war zone, flying actual missions. So I obtained permission from the Westover base commander to fly to North Africa to photograph our squadron in action. Our orders attached us to a squadron of B-24s that was about to embark.

The squadron's air base was located in Sbeitla, Tunisia, where an Air Force engineering battalion had performed the remarkable feat of building five landing fields in three days. The squadron also operated out of Ben Arouba, where in eight hours engineers had removed 1,788 mines from a single runway on a captured German base. These bases were located where Tunisia peaks into the Mediterranean, the closest point in Africa to Sicily and Italy. From that location, anti-submarine planes were also used to attack Fascist land positions.

I sent a message to Colonel Brackett informing him of our mission, but when we arrived, I discovered that he was on a special assignment at an air base outside London. Bad luck, because as far as his deputy was concerned—a dyspeptic major who was stressed trying to keep his planes on schedule—I was an unwelcome pain in the ass. He grudgingly agreed to let us accompany one mission, and then we were to get the hell off the air base. Walker was able to sandwich himself into the narrow B-25 nose beside the bombardier, but, limited to only one run, it was unlikely that we would get any useful footage.

We were fortunate with the weather. The morning of our mission was sparkling clear, and we were also lucky to have a laid-back crew that liked the notion of being filmed, especially the pilot, who asked me to take some footage of him at the controls to send to his wife in Tulsa. In all the many days of their search missions, the pilot told me, they had never sighted a U-boat or a tender, but, as luck would have it, in the last minutes of our flight, the cry of "Sub! Sub! Sub!" came from the flight deck. The plane went into a dive as the bombardier activated the bomb-bay doors. The B-25's speed got us to the sighting in seconds, and as we leveled off, the depth charges hit the surface, the plane pulling up sharply to avoid the concussive reaction as the charges roiled the water. We were too low on fuel to be able to circle the surface to look for telltale debris and an oil slick, but in getting footage of the actual bombing our mission was everything I had hoped for. We returned to Westover the following day.

Three days later, when the film came back from the developing lab, we excitedly projected it, but what we saw on the screen was not a view of the U-boat surface trail or of the exploding water. All we had was a blurred close-up of the bombardier's busy hands. Obviously, as combat cameraman, Sergeant Walker needed a little more work on his technique.

# Twelve

The time had come to pack up the very rough, very long assemblage we had made of our weeks of filming and take it out to Hollywood, where, with God's help, the First Motion Picture Unit of the United States Air Force might be able to make an acceptable movie out it. I wrote letters of approval for Sergeant Walker and Sergeant Brown, who returned to their units at Westover, and I boarded a Gettysburg-vintage Pullman car in New Jersey that carried me on a creeping, dismal journey to the coast via St. Louis, Kansas City, and El Paso.

The First Motion Picture Unit had been established by the Air Force in Culver City at the defunct but still well-equipped Hal Roach Studios. In these studios, Hal Roach had produced a wide variety of films, ranging from the "Our Gang" and Laurel and Hardy shorts to *Topper, Of Mice and Men,* and the special-effects extravaganza *One Million B.C.* Roach himself had been commissioned a colonel and functioned as liaison officer between the military and the Hollywood stars who were being directly commissioned by the Air Force to perform in this unit. Not only stars, but top writers, lighting technicians, sound engineers, set designers, gaffers, cameramen, and all the other vital Hollywood personnel were in uniform; the press referred to them as "celluloid cowboys."

The Hal Roach Studios were, in reality, Spanish-style, white stucco relics of the 1920s land boom, originally a boys' military academy prior to its acquisition by Roach, who added sound-stages and technical studios. The Air Force had in turn added hastily built barracks.

On my first day at Fort Roach, I was stunned at the sight of so many Hollywood stars like Captain Robert Sterling, Captain George Montgomery, Captain William Holden, and Second Lieutenant Ronald Reagan walking around in uniform. There were also enlisted men: Sergeant Lee J. Cobb, who was destined to play Willy Loman in *Death of a Salesman,* and Sergeant Arthur Kennedy, a remarkable stage actor who, twenty years later, played Nick Adams's father in a film I wrote, *Hemingway's Adventures of a Young Man.* The commander of Fort Roach was one of Hollywood's leading film directors, Frank Capra, who had been given a lieutenant colonel commission. Beginning in 1922, Capra had directed thirty films, among them such classics as *It Happened One Night, Mr. Deeds Goes to Town, Mr. Smith Goes to Washington,* and *Meet John Doe.* Soon after he left the service, Capra directed *It's a Wonderful Life,* which became a fixture in the panoply of enduring films.

Hollywood's connection with the military was nothing new, dating back to 1927 when military aviation combined with Hollywood's moviemakers to produce *Wings,* a silent film that won the first Academy Award for best motion picture.

The lot was bursting with activity. There was a unit staffed by combat camera crews in training. Another unit was devoted to the making of training films. Yet another worked with producers who were making feature films that had patriotic war themes; Colonel Jack Warner of Warner Bros. and the director Owen Crump were in charge of production. The writers' department was headed by First Lieutenant H. Clark Ramsey. Second in command was Lieutenant Richard Barr, who would become a venerable Broadway producer of such classics as *Sweeney Todd, The Grass Harp,* and *Who's Afraid of Virginia Woolf?*

After a couple of days I began to realize that despite all of Fort Roach's activity, it didn't translate into much production. There were constant conferences under the warm Hollywood sun, but the pace of production was more suited to the Warner Bros. lot than to the feverish pace of the war. But two important training films were produced while I was there: *Resisting Enemy Interrogation* and *Ditch and Live,* which dealt with crash survival.

I had to wait three days for a meeting with Colonel Capra, who, out of his pool of forty film editors, assigned to me a young GI named Jason Bernie, who had been a film editor at Columbia Pictures. He was the son of a very popular band leader, Ben Bernie, whose music originated in Chicago's College Inn and was broadcast over one of the major radio networks. Ben Bernie's signature was a growling "Yowsah, yowsah, yowsah." Private Jason was a handsome young man who had an urbanity, a civilized craftiness, that I admired. He was resentful at being relegated to the status of a buck-ass private when, in his words, "two-bit actors like Reagan have tin on their shoulders." I was assigned an editing room where I brought the reels of film we had clumsily spliced together. Jason took one glance at the mess and gave me a devastating look. "Make a film out of this? I'd rather be court-martialed."

But over the following weeks, slowly, methodically, thanks largely to Jason's skill, we began to assemble something presentable out of the mess we began with.

The Air Force had not commandeered a hotel in Los Angeles, so I had to find a place I could afford on my meager per diem. Many of the hotels offered discounts to servicemen and luckily I found a room at a shabby little hotel called the St. Moritz for an affordable three dollars a day. One of my favorite places for an evening's diversion was Slapsie Maxie's on Beverly Boulevard, where I could sit at the bar and watch the entertainment while nursing a drink (20 percent off for servicemen). Over a sixteen-year career as a light heavyweight, Slapsie Maxie Rosenbloom had fought hundreds of fights, sometimes fighting as often as four times a month. For four years he wore the crown as light heavyweight champion of the world, and later found a comedy niche in the movies by just being the slapsy person he was. Performing with him in a zany show were star comedians like Jackie Gleason, Ben Blue, Pat Moore, and Ben Lessey. Gleason, of course, had great postwar success on television with *The Honeymooners*. There were restaurants like Bill Jordan's that gave 15 percent deductions to men in uniform, and some theaters, the Turnabout on North La Cienega among them, that on certain nights admitted servicemen free of charge. The source for these Hollywood bonanzas was a booklet written by Staff Sergeant Frank Davidson, entitled *Where to Take Your Girl in L.A. on $1 to $20*. I had met a pretty girl named Judy Senter at the Officers' Club in Hollywood, and we took full advantage of Sergeant Davidson's research over the course of my Hollywood mission.

Jason Bernie had a narrow view of life that consisted of two objectives: making money to augment his meager GI salary and getting laid. On arrival every morning at our editing room, he would regale me with his frequent success at the latter, but freelancing additional income was not going as well, a fact that fed his churlishness about the mean task I had handed him. Takes didn't match, exposures had considerable variations, and intended sequences were often not sequential. I had given the movie a pretentious title, *Atlantic Mission*, and I hoped that the dramatic, bombastic narration that I had written would cover some of the cinematic defects. It was vital, therefore, that the narrator bring a dramatic quality to the soundtrack.

I put in my narrator request to Colonel Capra, who had a large pool of commissioned Hollywood actors to draw from, but I certainly wasn't prepared for the GI who reported to me—Alan Ladd. Having recently seen him in *This Gun for Hire* in the Westover movie theater, I was startled by the disparity between the tough guy of the silver screen and the figure who came sauntering through the door. In the flesh, he couldn't have been more than five feet two in his tailored uniform, and he had orange-blond hair.

"What's up, kid?" were the first words out of the mouth of Alan Ladd addressing his superior officer, Lieutenant Hotchner.

Speechless, I handed him the script. He lit a cigarette while he glanced at the first page.

"Boring shit, ain't it?" he said.

We walked across the lot to the building where the recording studio was located, Ladd turning pages en route.

"Let's get this over with, Vern," Ladd said to the sergeant behind glass in the control room. Ladd sat down at the mike and in a monotone mumble began to read my script as if it were an obituary. He was rushing through it, but I sure as hell wasn't going to tell Alan Ladd, movie star, to slow down. He monotoned on for about twenty minutes, at which time he glanced at his Rolex and announced that he had a lunch date at the Brown Derby. "We'll wipe it up in the morning," he said as he cocked his hat over one eye, lit another cigarette, and departed. The engineer handed me the recording, which I took back to our editing room. Jason set up the recorder, and Ladd's voice filled the room. I listened with mounting apprehension.

"Jason," I said, "are you listening to this?"

"Yeah."

"Do you hear what I hear?"

"What?"

"Has he got a hitch—I mean like his tongue is catching on his teeth? He sounds more like a stickup man than the voice of the Air Force."

Jason listened. "You can't use it."

"But all those movies of his . . ."

"Yeah, but on the screen I guess it's not so noticeable."

"What am I going to do?"

"Can him. Get someone else."

"*I* am going to fire Alan Ladd?"

"You're a lieutenant, Lieutenant. He's not Alan Ladd, movie star, he's a fucking, buck-ass private, getting twenty-one dollars a month, same as me."

That evening, I nervously rehearsed with Judy how I would adroitly handle Ladd in the morning. The rehearsal didn't help. Ladd was in a foul mood when he walked into the studio, no good morning or any of that, and plopped himself down at the mike.

"Where's that crap I'm reading?" he asked.

I was nervous as hell. "Ladd . . . Private Ladd . . . about the script . . . I mean, I know you're busy and so . . . well, it's such a long script . . ."

"No speeches, kid, just give me the goddamn script."

"That's just it."

"What's just it?"

"There is no script."

"You're not doing the flick?"

"Well, I'm arranging . . . I mean . . . somebody else is going to . . . you know, read it . . ."

Ladd swiveled his head around to look at me, astonished, then started laughing. "I'll be a son of a bitch," he sputtered, choking on his laughter as he slammed his way out the door. I felt like I had survived a mortar burst.

From the control booth, Vern, the engineer, spoke to me over the intercom. "Nice going, Lieutenant," he said, giving me a thumbs-up sign through the glass.

As to be expected, my rejection of Ladd did not diminish his postwar career. Between 1945 and 1964 he made forty-three films, with *Shane* as his crowning achievement. In 1979, I wrote a biography of Sophia Loren, who told me that costarring with Ladd in *Boy on a Dolphin* was the most unpleasant experience of her career, and she had made seventy-four films. I sympathized with her.

To replace Ladd, Capra sent me an actor named John Beal, who had performed on Broadway and in such films as *Les Miserables* and *The Little Minister*. He read the narration superbly and did not call me "kid."

# Thirteen

Converting raw film footage into a finished picture with integrated sound and titles took much longer than I had anticipated, so I had a lot of time on my hands. I knew no one in Hollywood but there was one man I was anxious to meet, my uncle Henry Hotchener, who had not dropped the middle *e* from his name as my father had. My father had often told me about the famous coastal Hotcheners: Maurice in New York and Henry in Los Angeles. Maurice had been the attorney for Jimmy Walker, the flamboyant New York mayor of the twenties (Maurice's official title was Special Corporation Counsel of the City of New York), and Henry had been the business manager and confidant of the incomparable actor John Barrymore.

When I was in New York on my way to Westover Field, I had gone to see Maurice Hotchener, who was then in private practice. He was a diminutive, natty gentleman, bow tie and vest, who was having his shoes shined by an itinerant bootblack when I was ushered into his office. He offered me a shine, and while our shoes were being glossed he gave me a capsule summary of the family history of the Hotcheners and the Hotchners, calling one "the *e* clan" and the other "the pretenders." I found him witty and amusing, especially when he spoke about the Jimmy Walker days. He opened a drawer and showed me one of his Walker mementos—a peculiarly shaped piece of iron with an electrical cord attached to it which Walker had invented so that his valet could iron the shoulders and back of Walker's suit jackets after he had put them on, thereby molding them to his body. "Nattiest dresser I ever met," my Uncle Maurice said, with admiration. "As soon as I can afford a valet, I'll start using the iron."

I asked him about his brother Henry; he told me that when Barrymore was alive, Henry often asked him to do legal work for Barrymore. Maurice said that Henry and his wife, Marie, had been close associates of Barrymore for seventeen years, right up to his death, which had occurred only a few months before our meeting.

Both Henry and Marie were deeply involved in the occult and in after-death phenomena, and they had actually met while on a psychic journey to India. My Aunt Marie was, according to Maurice, an authority on theosophy and abnormal psychic phenomena as well as an extraordinary astrologer. Henry and Marie had been to India many times, taking Barrymore with them on one occasion, and Marie had participated in psychotherapeutic experiments conducted by the leading occult scientists of the day in clinics in Nancy and the Salpétriére in Paris.

Henry and Marie had been educated in American schools. Henry studied law at Georgetown University and the University of Southern California; Marie, after her graduation from Mills College in Oakland, showed great promise as a soprano, performing operatic roles in Italy, France, and Germany, often with the composer Puccini himself conducting the orchestra. But her interest in theosophy and spiritual phenomena eventually possessed her and she turned down all operatic engagements, including an invitation from Frau Cosima Wagner to sing at the Bayreuth Festival.

"They had enormous influence on Jack Barrymore," Maurice said. "He was dependent on Henry for business affairs, and he wouldn't make a move until Marie checked it out on her astrological calendar. You must go see them. They live in an area north of Franklin Avenue that they are developing as a real estate venture."

There was no telephone listed for Henry Hotchener at the address Maurice had given me; the two letters I had written to him had gone unanswered, so one afternoon, having nothing better to do, I decided to go and knock on my uncle's door.

The area in which he lived was north of Hollywood Boulevard, a section where there had not been much development. I had difficulty finding the house, which, as it turned out, stood far back from a massive, rusted, iron gate. There was a bell on the gate but it was rusted beyond usefulness. The gate was slightly ajar, however, and it opened with a painful squeal. I self-consciously walked up the winding drive to the house, its facade as unkempt as the weed-covered lawns and the decrepit driveway. All the blinds on the windows were shut. I seriously doubted that my uncle and aunt, or anyone else, lived there.

I rang the bell and heard it sound shrilly in the interior. No answer. I rang again, and again, and was preparing to leave when I heard a slight rustle from within, followed by a clank of the door's protective metal. I was confronted with a man, or, to be more precise, an apparition, for this individual was dressed like a genie, a green genie, in a silk tunic and silk blousy pants tapering into Arabian pointed, jeweled slippers, a wide beaded and bejeweled belt around his waist, a huge gold scarab on a chain at his neck, and, incongruously, a tennis visor on his forehead. He looked at me, saying nothing.

"I'm . . . ah . . . Lieutenant Hotchner. I came to see my Uncle Henry if he's here . . ." The man put a finger to his lips, even though I had spoken in a low voice, and he gestured for me to follow him. The house was dimly lit and smelled of incense and musk. I followed him across a foyer and into what I supposed was the dining room, but in the center of the room, in place of a dining table, there was an Indian funeral bier with a stout woman, shrouded in a flowing white gown, stretched out on it. Her hair and her complexion were as white as her gown. Her eyes were closed and her arms were crossed over her ample chest. A band of jewels encircled her forehead, and a scarab, identical to the one worn by the man, hung from a gold chain around her neck.

The man stopped at the bier and said: "Dear, this is Sam Hotchner's boy, now a lieutenant in the Air Force. This is my wife, Marie," he said, quite formally.

I managed to extract a "How do you do?" out of my throat, but Aunt Marie did not move or reply. She wasn't dead, however, for I distinctly saw the rise and fall of her copious bosom. I guessed her to be at least twenty years older than my uncle.

He now led me through the dining room and into a butler's pantry, where he motioned for us to sit on two high stools that he placed close to each other. He spoke to me in a very low voice, so as not to disturb his wife, I presumed. He asked about my father, whom he had not seen in twenty years, and then he asked me what I was doing in Hollywood. He knew about the First Motion Picture Unit, because, he said, in his long association with Barrymore he had become familiar with all the Hollywood studios. I told him that John Barrymore was the greatest actor I had ever seen. My uncle said that it was difficult for him to talk about Jack because he had just died the previous May, and it was painful to mention his name, so much did my uncle love him. My uncle said that his wife had been so affected by Barrymore's death that she had been in a spiritual trance ever since. She was one of the world's greatest astrologers, he said, and Barrymore would always consult her before going on a trip or making a movie or getting involved with a woman. She once warned him, based on his astrological chart, not to drive his automobile on a particular day, but he forgot, his car went off the road and turned over, and he suffered a concussion and a fractured hip. He became so dependent on Marie's readings that he would not shoot an important scene in a picture without first checking the astrological signs with her.

My uncle said they had taken Barrymore on a trip to India at a time when his health was beginning to fail and alcoholism was getting the better of him. At first the ayurvedic cure, which was given by a Dr. Murti and involved herbs and essences from the Himalayas, seemed to work, but after a couple of weeks Barrymore suddenly disappeared. They later discovered he had bought out an Indian brothel stocked with Eurasian girls, spent a week there, and between the bar and the obliging girls undid all the good the cure had done him.

I sat there all afternoon on that stool in the butler's pantry, listening to my uncle's Barrymore stories, oblivious of time, feeling sad and empty when he got to the end of Barrymore's life and described the painful and miserable way he had died, his mind and body in ruins from years of abuse.

I wanted to ask Uncle Henry so many things but we were both suddenly startled by a shrill sound that came from the dining room. My uncle immediately got off his stool and said I would have to be leaving. As we passed Aunt Marie I heard her droning a litany of strange sounds, perhaps a Hindu prayer from the way it sounded.

At the door, my uncle gave me a card on which his name and address were printed. "Tell your father," he said, "that we are developing this entire area. There's not much here now but after the war people will start to build here and he can make his fortune. I've heard how bad things were for him and your family during the Depression, but this is his chance to recoup. We have building lots here for as little as a hundred dollars. Tell him. I'd like to see you again while you are here, perhaps entertain you, but you see how things are . . ."

He quickly closed the door.

I wrote to my father about Henry's offer and enclosed his card, but my father's response was that he didn't put money in get-rich-quick schemes. Of course, my father had no money, and even if he had he would have invested it in something that was a sure loser. My father had a limitless capacity for failure.

# Fourteen

All the artwork for the title and credits was in the works, but *Atlantic Mission* was desperately in need of whatever help it could get from music.

"I'll call Davey Rose," Jason said. David Rose was a composer, conductor, and arranger who, prior to joining the service, had been music director for the Mutual Broadcasting System. He had done arrangements for many of the big-band leaders, including Benny Goodman, Glenn Miller, and Jason's father. At present he was in charge of the Air Force Orchestra at the Santa Ana Air Base—forty soldier-musicians who had previously played for some of the country's leading symphony and jazz orchestras, and a distinguished symphonic harpist, Mary Cambern.

Lieutenant David Rose was a pleasant, unassuming man who screened my film sympathetically and recorded a soaring score that made full use of his forty-one instruments. His forceful rendition of the Air Force anthem "Wild Blue Yonder" for the opening credits really got the film into the wild blue.

My Hollywood sojourn was nearing its end, and about time. As our armed forces grew in personnel and equipment, we were beginning to assert ourselves, and I wanted to rejoin my squadron and be in on it. Isolated as I was among the palm trees and movie glitter of Hollywood, I was experiencing the same feeling that had depressed me toward the end of *Three Dots with a Dash,* a feeling akin to embarrassment bordering on shame that I was not performing what I regarded as my war duty. I desperately wanted to participate in the heroics of our troops as reported in the daily papers, and I counted the days until I could get back to New York, deliver the film, and quickly rejoin my outfit in North Africa. Determined to avoid another eternal train ride across the country, I was able to snag a ride with a B-24 camera crew that was headed for the Eighth Air Force in England with a refueling stop in New York.

I presented my can of film to General Larson's deputy colonel, who instructed me to stand by for an official screening for the general and his staff. For two weeks I stood by with mounting apprehension that another show business project might be thrust upon me. Well, not this time, I told myself, and I rehearsed my speech: "I am wearing this uniform for military duty, not to make musicals or movies, but to make war. My place is with my outfit in North Africa, fighting the Nazis, and that's where I want to go." As the days went on and I sat alone in my deserted Church Street movie office biding my time, I became increasingly apprehensive that derailment might be on the way.

The unveiling of *Atlantic Mission* finally took place in the navy's auditorium in the Church Street building. General Larson and his staff of about fifty officers attended, as did an admiral and a large contingent of naval personnel. I was surprised by the attendance since I had had no idea that the screening was going to be anything more than an intimate viewing for the general and a few aides. As the film got under way, I sat to one side where I could watch the audience's reactions, but to my dismay there were none. The officers kept their eyes focused on the screen, their faces expressionless. They did not move, cough, scratch, look at each other, or show any signs that they liked or disliked what they saw.

With the crescendoing musical finale from David Rose's minions, the film ended, the lights came back on, General Larson arose, and, without looking at his men (or at me), his face blank, left the auditorium, followed by the scowling admiral and his entourage. What the hell, was there a military regulation against applauding? The projectionist handed me the reels, not bothering to rewind them. I felt utterly defeated, and by the time I got back to my office a really grim possibility had presented itself: what if the general, obviously not thrilled with what he saw, ordered me to redo the film according to a list his staff had prepared, this time doing this, that, and the other thing? Back into production with Sergeant Walker and Sergeant Brown, back in Hollywood with Jason Bernie, back in my St. Moritz cell. Not a matter of choice, for if I refused, the only alternative was a court-martial, which would get me to the brig, not North Africa.

I didn't sleep much that night. The following morning, I dragged my enervated body into my office and there on my desk was a large envelope bearing the imprimatur of General Larson. I didn't want to open it, convinced that it was bad news because if he had had anything favorable to say he would surely have summoned me to his office.

I finally stopped procrastinating and fearfully removed the contents of the envelope. It contained three things: (1) an order to provide anti-submarine headquarters with two hundred prints of *Atlantic Mission*; (2) a letter signed by the general and addressed to me: "The significant submarine accomplishments by the Air Force have not received deserved recognition. This film will give us the favorable attention we deserve. I enter a commendation into your record, along with a promotion in rank to first lieutenant"; and (3) a directive promoting me to the rank of first lieutenant.

It took about a week to wind myself through the layers of red tape required to obtain the two hundred copies. I had contacted Westover Field and learned that I would be attached to a transport flight that was scheduled for the Sbeitla air base in Tunisia. I had replaced my gold bars with silver (only in the military is silver more precious than gold), my pay envelope was a bit fatter, and I was able to celebrate my success with a very attractive Dutch ballet dancer I had met named Tina DeRoos, whose troupe had been stranded in New York when Hitler invaded Holland. She would be good company until I left for North Africa to join up with the U-boat killers of the 13th Wing.

# Fifteen

The directive was hand-delivered by a command corporal: all officers were to report to General Larson's briefing room, Mitchel Field, at 0900. (Mitchel Field, located at Hempstead, Long Island, was the headquarters of the anti-submarine command.) That evening, Tina and I went to see a Broadway musical, and I had no presentiment of the doom that was looming at 0900.

"Gentlemen," General Larson said, "the Joint Chiefs have reorganized the overall anti-submarine command, and henceforth all anti-submarine missions will be transferred to the Navy, which thereby removes the anti-submarine command of the Air Force from the table of organization. We are directed to wind down our operation within thirty days. Those of you who command units at Westover Field and 90 Church Street must take immediate steps to dissolve your units."

An officer rose from his seat. "General, sir, question, please."

"Yes, Major Wheland."

"Does this mean that we will have specific reassignments or are we simply cut loose?"

"Unfortunately, Major, you are all unemployed, so to speak, and after your thirty days to wind down your operations you then have an additional thirty days to affiliate yourself with another Air Force unit or you will be assigned to the redistribution center in Atlantic City, New Jersey, for reevaluation and reassignment."

The dreaded repo-depot was where incompetent officers were assigned to be redeployed, primarily to mess halls, garages, sanitation units, and the like in remote outposts in the Pacific.

"All planes, flight equipment, and armaments," the general

continued, "will be taken over by the First Bomber Command, but you will be responsible for distributing all other equipment and supplies in the possession of your units. Colonel Harlow Peters is in charge of the distribution and will be available for consultation. Anything further?"

I stood up. "General Larson, what shall I do with the two hundred movie prints you ordered?"

"Hand them around as souvenirs." Then in a sarcastic tone, "Maybe Admiral McQuale would like one to see how it's done—he's taking over from us."

There were more questions but I stopped listening. Five times now, five times on the brink of going to war only to be blindsided by the fickle finger of military fate, as if some fairy goon were hovering over me intent on whacking me every time I tried to get going: faulty depth perception, flat feet, musical comedy, movie, and now unemployment. Whack! Whack! Whack! On top of it, I had only thirty days to somehow get rid of over a million dollars' worth of movie equipment. And to make matters worse, the Navy sent out a directive that all Air Force space at 90 Church Street was needed for their personnel and that the contents of all Air Force offices were being moved to Mitchel Field.

From what I subsequently learned, for months there had been an ongoing struggle between the Air Force and the Navy over anti-submarine activity. The Navy resented the Air Force operating over water, which they felt was the Navy's prerogative. But the Air Force insisted that aerial reconnaissance was *their* prerogative. I even heard that the Navy resented *Atlantic Mission* as a final intolerable usurpation of their sovereignty. If so, then I was the final straw that grounded the Air Force, thereby ironically destroying my chance to go to Tunisia and finally get involved in combat.

I thought the first of my tasks would be easy—simply inform the Air Force supply depot at Dayton that I was returning to them all the equipment and provisions they had issued to me. No, Dayton responded, we are an issuing organization with no authority to receive and recycle returns. But what will I do with all this stuff? We suggest you find some Air Force outfit that needs it.

So there I was at a strange Air Force base on Long Island with a mountain of rather valuable equipment that had to be disposed of in thirty days. The first thing I did was to canvass a variety of military units with activities that might possibly tie in with this equipment: the Signal Corps, the First Motion Picture Unit, Aerial Reconnaissance, *Air Force Magazine, Stars and Stripes,* the public-relations branches of the three services, and so forth, but none of them showed any interest in anything on my list. I was a traveling salesman, showing photos of my wares. Unlike the Elgin watches my father peddled in his territory, my wares were free-of-charge. But I wasn't doing any better than my father, who, during the Depression, was trying to sell watches to people who were struggling to put food on their tables.

It was ironic that now, when I desperately needed to be rescued—I'd settle for a musical, a movie, a book, whatever—no such thing was in sight. I had nightmare visions of myself in charge of a mess hall at an Air Force base on New Guinea, commanding a squad of potato-peeling GIs, or as a recreation officer in charge of Ping-Pong and shuffleboard at the R&R center in Albuquerque. I had recently received an APO letter from my old friend Chris Donohue, who was commander of a PT boat in the South Pacific, telling me how he had been rescued at sea after his boat was sunk by a direct hit from a Jap destroyer: just the sort of heroic action I had envisioned when he and I had gone for our V-12 physical, but which had been denied to me because of my lamentable feet. I hadn't heard from Myron Gollub, but I imagined him performing heroics, zooming off flight decks in his navy fighter. And here I was, peddling cameras and Photostat machines and trying to avoid the fatal clutch of the repo-depot.

After two weeks of futilely searching for some outfit to take the stuff off my hands, in desperation I resorted to staging a sidewalk sale. Mitchel Field, a long-established base devoted to flight training, had family housing for its permanent cadre. So I filled the area in front of my ground-level storage facility with those items that I thought might have family appeal—the refrigerators, cameras, film, desks, chairs, bookcases, and the like—each item bearing a sign that read "Yours for the Taking." Like a shill at a circus sideshow, I stood on the sidewalk hawking my wares to passing officers, GIs, wives, civilian employees, children, anybody. "Take a look, folks, absolutely free of charge. Need a refrigerator? How about a nice movie camera with lots of film? Need a desk or a chair, how about a nice table for your kitchen? Wouldn't you like a projector and a screen to watch your home movies—all free, just walk up and tote 'em away!"

Passersby were initially wary of my giveaway, but once I started to get customers and word got around, I did a pretty brisk business disposing of items that could be used in the family houses. I cornered those who took the 16mm projectors and tried to get them to take one of my stack of *Atlantic Missions*, but there were no takers. I could understand that when someone was on Air Force duty all day, the last thing he wanted was to spend the evening watching a film about the Air Force.

Despite my sidewalk success, I was still saddled with all the big, expensive equipment. I consulted Colonel Peters about the surplus. He pointed out that since these items had been issued in my name and I had personally signed for them, I could be held accountable for them by the Air Force Inspector General. While I was at it, I asked Colonel Peters if there was a possibility that he could help get me into a unit that was actively engaged in combat. I told him how much it meant to me, how it had eluded me.

"Lieutenant," he said, "there are four hundred anti-submarine officers making the same request. It's a sad situation, but all Air Force outfits are reporting that their tables of organization are full up. Looks like you'll have to face the repo-depot crapshoot with all the others unless you have a buddy in command somewhere. Maybe someone from your OCS class."

On the next to last day of my grace period, I received a call from the supply sergeant I had spoken to at *Air Force Magazine,* the official magazine of the Air Force, summoning me for an appointment the following morning. I presumed they had changed their minds and decided to take my extensive lab equipment since they used a considerable number of photos in their monthly issues.

*Air Force Magazine* headquarters was located in a high-rise office building at One Park Avenue, a few blocks south of Grand Central Station. The civilian receptionist, an attractive woman in a flowered dress, informed me that I was to meet with Colonel James H. Straubel, the editor-in-chief. I wondered why the editor was getting involved when a supply sergeant could easily sign on for my stuff. In fact, I wondered why I'd been summoned— all they had to do was send a truck and load up whatever they wanted.

I passed by a series of desks on my way to Colonel Straubel's office, personnel ranging from corporals to majors, busily typing. Lieutenant Colonel Harry Russell, the deputy editor, ushered me into Colonel Straubel's office, announcing me in the process, but Colonel Straubel was engrossed with what he was reading and did not even acknowledge me. What he was reading was my classification card, that blasted albatross that was permanently hung around my neck next to my dog tag.

The colonel was a burly, balding man who had two crooked fingers on his left hand. "You're a lawyer," he said, his eyes on the card.

"Yes, sir."

"You've done a musical for Sheppard Field, a movie for Anti-Sub . . ."

"Yes, sir."

"You've dealt with film, enlargements, prints?"

"Yes, sir."

"Well, Lieutenant," he said, putting down the card and looking at me for the first time, "we're not interested in any of your equipment—we don't do our own photography—but we are interested in you. We don't have a photo editor and, as a consequence, we don't get quality photos. You think you could handle the job? You'll have to spend a lot of time in D.C., mostly the Pentagon, see if you can cultivate some good sources, and write captions. How's that strike you?"

"Oh, just fine, sir—fine." Little did he know that if he had asked me to get shot out of a cannon straight to the Pentagon, the answer would have been the same.

"One more prerequisite, very important. Most of the really good shots, especially the aerials, are routinely stamped 'classified,' meaning we can't use 'em. So your job—get hold of the peacheroos and try to get them declassified. Might be tricky—think you can handle that? You'll have to cultivate good relationships with Pentagon people."

And so, once more, my classification card had controlled my military destiny, but this time with no regrets from me. I added up the cost of all the equipment I was leaving at Mitchel Field, and it came to $980,000, for which the inspector general could hold me personally liable. War is full of risks, I told myself as I packed up my gear and headed to New York City.

# Sixteen

Colonel Straubel gave me ten days to settle in before reporting for duty. My first order of business was to liberate myself from my monastery-like room at the Henry Hudson Hotel. On the bulletin board of the Officers' Club at the Commodore Hotel, I got the name of a Captain Sidney Schwartz, who was a dentist attached to a medical unit on Staten Island. He was looking for an officer to share his small, furnished, two-bedroom apartment in the Wentworth, a run-down, dreary complex in the theater district opposite the Martin Beck Theatre. Captain Schwartz, an amiable, talkative fellow, had sublet the apartment from an actor who had gone to Hollywood. The furniture looked like it had been used by a *Tobacco Road* touring company; the mohair chairs and sofa, greased by many a leaning head, had springs pushing against the surface like ribs in a starving hound dog. The windows faced other windows, and the bed in my room—which, of course, was considerably smaller than Schwartz's—had a center slant that was a valley between two mountains. The grease on the kitchen stove had been baked into a ceramic-like coating, and the chipped dishes were strangers to each other.

Nevertheless I moved in, because wartime New York City had no vacancies I could conceivably afford. Large sums of money were paid under the table just to have access to negotiating for a rental. Landlords had more clout than the mayor. So, prudently, despite my misgivings, I resigned myself to accepting my fate as Captain Schwartz's roommate, but, as it turned out, not for long. Captain Schwartz had certain peculiarities that put an immediate strain on our cohabitation. To begin with, he had a portable phonograph on which he played an endless succession of Shirley Temple recordings. In the morning, while he brushed his teeth and showered, he played "On the Good Ship Lollipop," Shirley Temple's cute little voice filling the apartment. When he returned in the evening, *every* evening, the Shirley Temple musicale began with "Animal Crackers in My Soup," accompanied by some Shirley tap-tap-tapping. I pointed out to Schwartzie that a little of little Shirley was more than enough for me, and he promised to turn the volume down, but faint Shirley was no improvement over Shirley in full throttle. The real hell of it was that a Shirley refrain would get in my head and stay there all day long. "Animal crackers in my soup, Monkeys and rabbits loop the loop, Gosh, oh gee, but I have fun . . ." Over and over again, all day long, no way to banish it, monkeys and rabbits loop the loop the loop the loop the loop the loop the loop . . .

Schwartzie often came back to the apartment late at night with various young women who seemed to be members of the Shirley Temple Fan Club, the way they shared his enthusiasm for her cute little ditties, an enthusiasm that also embraced his canteen booze. Jim Beam or Southern Comfort plus several choruses of "Polly-Wolly-Doodle" or "You've Gotta Eat Your Spinach, Baby" or "You've Gotta S-M-I-L-E to Be H-A-Double-P-Y," and Shirley would be joined by the rhythmic creaking of Captain Schwartz's bedsprings and moans that didn't come from Shirley. I couldn't figure out what there was about "Ride a Cock-Horse" or "Oh, My Goodness" that turned women on, but I grudgingly had to admire Schwartzie's success rate.

I occasionally escaped Shirley by spending the night with Tina, but I was desperate to get my own digs before settling into my new job. Tina wanted me to move in with her but she lived in a tiny studio and, besides, the Air Force required proof of a self-maintained residence to qualify for the per diem additional pay granted to personnel stationed in New York City. Tina lived on

Christopher Street in Greenwich Village, a neighborhood I much preferred to the Wentworth's Eighth Avenue area, where I ran a gauntlet of whores and hustlers every night. But I got a break one night when Tina invited me to a party given by a friend of hers, Bernadine Inzoraan.

Bernadine was an attractive woman of thirty or so with a shock of the most lustrous amber hair imaginable. Her narrow house on Wooster Street, four stories high, was adjacent to a stable that housed a dozen of the nags that pulled carriages in Central Park. In the course of the evening, Tina discovered that Bernadine had a barren room on the fourth floor off a hallway that also gave onto a small bathroom. I said it would be fine but that I had no furniture. Bernadine said that was not a problem—she would throw a furniture party for me. In the hallway outside the room there were stacks of tiles that Bernadine had hand-painted and baked in her kiln (she was a well-known ceramic artist), and she said that if I could manage with all the tiles stored there, the apartment was mine for fifty dollars a month.

I enjoyed living there. The furniture party provided me with more than enough domestic comforts (in fact, I had a surplus that I donated to the Salvation Army). The flat itself was only three blocks away from Tina's place, and it was easy to get to Thirty-third and Park, where the *Air Force* offices were located.

Bernadine's husband, Alain, was in the Merchant Marine on the run to Murmansk and appeared infrequently. Her mother, an imposing, imperial woman known as "The White Princess," was a Russian émigré who dressed only in white and was disposed toward reciting dramatic accounts of her czarist days.

Once every month, like clockwork, Bernadine gave a cocktail soiree to which I was invariably invited. Russian delicacies were served under the supervision of the White Princess, a string trio played Mozart, and the guests were an attractive, homogeneous mix of Village artists and well-heeled foreigners with exotic accents. I was the only one there in uniform, but Bernadine made a point of introducing me to people, thereby making me feel at ease in the group.

Those times when Alain Inzoraan came back from the sea, he often took stacks of Bernadine's tiles with him on his return trip to Russia. Using superlatives drenched with her thick accent, the White Princess extolled the popularity of her daughter's tiles in the Soviet Union, describing her as an artist whose tiles spoke "to the core of Russian souls."

I stayed in the Wooster Street apartment for over a year, but after I left to go overseas I never again visited the house, nor did I ever again see Bernadine, the White Princess, Tina, or any of the people I used to see at the soirees. But many years after the war ended, the Wooster Street house came back into my life when I was visited by two FBI agents.

"When you were in the Air Force, did you not live in Greenwich Village on Wooster Street in the house of one Bernadine Inzoraan?" one of them asked me.

"Yes."

"That's what we'd like to ask you about."

"About Bernadine?"

"Well, about that house, everything about it."

I didn't think there was much to tell them, but I described how Tina had introduced me and how my apartment had been furnished by contributions and about the monthly soirees. They said they were interested in some of the guests who attended those soirees, and they handed me a stack of photographs, asking me to indicate the ones whom I recognized. I said I couldn't do that unless I knew precisely what they were looking for.

"The house on Wooster Street has been torn down," one of the agents said, "but we have developed reliable information that it was the focal point of espionage activities of Russian agents during the war. Bernadine Inzoraan was the coordinator, and the so-called White Princess, who, in fact, was not Mrs. Inzoraan's mother, was in charge of the operation. The house on Wooster Street was used as a monthly drop by various Soviet spies in the New York-Washington area. They would come to those monthly cocktail parties for the dual purpose of leaving material to be couriered to Moscow and to get new instructions. The mix of people that Mrs. Inzoraan provided was perfect cover for their operation, and having you there in your Air Force uniform was very useful."

"Now about those tiles that were stored outside your door," the other agent continued, "they contained some of the most sensitive information that the Russian agents were able to obtain during those years. The espionage reports that were left with the White Princess at the parties were put on microfilm and then baked into those tiles by Bernadine Inzoraan. Then Mr. Inzoraan would take them with him on his trips to Murmansk, where they were delivered to the KGB."

By this time my mind was reeling from these revelations; I always felt that there was something strange about those soirees, repeated in precise thirty-day cycles and, considering the difficulty of obtaining wartime comestibles, so lavish. But all that was not so strange that it aroused my suspicions. I suppose any suspicions that might have formed were allayed by the eccentricity of the White Princess, who was the personification of the Madwoman of Chaillot in the celebrated play by Jean Giraudoux.

I looked through the stack of photographs, some of which were blurred and indistinct, taken, perhaps, with undercover cameras. Some of the faces were familiar, regulars who came to the cocktail parties every month. There was a photo of a man and woman, smiling, that the agents were particularly interested in. Yes, I was sure that they were there quite often. No, I didn't know their names, but they were certainly part of the group. One of the

agents turned the photograph over and showed me the names on
the back: Sobell, Morton, and Sobell, Helen. Morton Sobell had
been revealed to be a key confederate in the notorious Rosenberg
conspiracy.

The agents did not reveal any of the other identities. They
marked those photos that I recognized and thanked me for my
cooperation. I asked what had happened to the Inzoraans and the
White Princess; they said the FBI had been searching for them but
could not find a trace of them, and it was presumed that they had
long ago defected to Russia.

After the FBI men departed, I sat at my desk for a while thinking
about those parties, trying to remember any incidents that in ret-
rospect seemed strange. Then I remembered something. Tina and
I had been invited to a birthday party. Phil Thompson's birthday.
Phil had gone to Washington University with me; married now,
with a couple of babies, he lived in a garden apartment in the
Village. His obesity and high blood pressure had disqualified him
for military service and he was prospering as an account executive
with the advertising firm of Young & Rubicam.

We were late for the birthday party ("a surprise, so please be
on time") and I had neglected to get a present. As I left my room,
some of Bernadine's newest, most colorful tiles struck my eye. I
thought Bernadine might sell me a couple to give to good old Phil
for his birthday. I stopped downstairs to ask her but she was out,
so I went ahead and took a couple of tiles. I didn't see Bernadine
for several weeks—she was out of town—and I forgot about those
tiles. Phil Thompson died shortly after the war, and I had no idea
what had become of his family. But I now began to fantasize about
what priceless microfilms might have been in those two tiles that I
gave him. Perhaps by pinching those tiles I had prevented Russia
from obtaining a Pentagon blueprint for a new fighter plane or
from being able to break our code.

The way I eventually worked it out in my own mind, I was a hero for having prevented those two tiles from getting to the Russians; but in my heart I knew I had been a naive dupe for a couple of clever spies who ran their operation right under the nose of Lieutenant A. E. Hotchner of the United States Air Force.

# Seventeen

*Air Force Magazine* was a slick-paper publication that was comparable in general appearance and amount of editorial content to general magazines of national circulation. Approximately 550,000 copies of *Air Force* were shipped to AAF installations throughout the world, where they were locally circulated so that each magazine was read by four or five GIs. It was distributed free of charge, carried no ads, and was written by an Air Force staff who, as civilians, had been professional writers. As combat correspondents, these writers covered both war theaters, either on special assignments or attached to overseas units for the express purpose of covering the air war for the magazine. To gather their information, they flew numerous combat missions in virtually every combat area. One correspondent had flown the first five successive low-level B-29 missions against Japan from Guam. Another bailed out of a flaming C-47 transport over Germany during an airborne attack and joined an infantry outfit to help take an enemy position.

As I read articles in the back copies of the magazine, I realized that if I could prove myself as a writer, there was a real possibility of getting assigned to cover these combat activities. In those initial days at the magazine, I was impressed by how concentrated the writers were on the copy they were producing. I presumed they were writing vivid accounts of their exploits on combat missions flown over Germany, Italy, and targets in the Pacific.

But then I met the writers and discovered that the clatter of their typewriter keys was not fully devoted to chronicling the heroic actions of the Air Force. Major Luther Davis was writing a play titled *Kiss Them for Me* that was destined for Broadway with Judy Holliday in the performance that first made her famous. Staff Sergeant Ed Wallace, formerly a feature writer for the *World-Telegram,* was at work on an autobiographical novel, *Barrington,* that would eventually be published by Simon & Schuster. Sergeant Peter Bowman, who had never been in combat, was writing a long, narrative combat poem entitled *Beach Red* that would become a selection of the Book-of-the-Month Club. Staff Sergeant Mark Murphy, formerly of *The New Yorker,* was at work on a profile for that magazine. Sergeant Irving Kolodin, previously the music critic for the *Journal-American,* was now spending much of his time editing questions for the highly popular radio quiz show *Information Please.* Major Arthur Gordon, the prewar managing editor of *Good Housekeeping* magazine, was busy writing a novel that would eventually be published as *Reprisal.* And so on.

But these men would periodically go off on assignments, usually attaching themselves to an Air Force combat unit, and write very effective articles about their missions: "Blocking Back in a P-47," by Major Gordon, who accompanied Thunderbolt fighter planes protecting bombers over Germany; Major Davis's "The G Stands for Guts," about a unit of fifty-three gliders silently descending behind Japanese lines in Burma; Sergeant Murphy's "Troubleshooters," a firsthand description of P-47s protecting flak-damaged B-17s over Germany—articles that covered virtually every aspect of AAF combat around the world, all of them reflecting the active participation of their writers.

Each week I took the train to Washington, D.C., which at that time was even more overcrowded than New York. The mass of military personnel that was packed into the city gave the impression that everyone in Washington was in uniform. There were not nearly enough buildings to house the expanded military presence and all the new agencies that had been created to deal with the war, so temporary crude wooden shacks and trailers had been set up in open spaces all over the capital, giving it the atmosphere of a bustling frontier mining town. All the parks, malls, and open grounds were covered by these structures. I spent most of my time at the Pentagon, which was still under construction. After a few weeks of indoctrination, I was able to establish fairly good rapport with a couple of officers in the Air Force photo section. Since I represented the Air Force's own magazine, they would give me my pick of the most recent aerial photos and photos of related airfield activity and I would write captions based on information that accompanied the photos. I was even able to promote a pass for the War Room, where I had access to inside information. On days when I was in the Park Avenue offices, I began to be given inconsequential writing assignments—short items, editing letters from readers, copyreading—a variety of chores that I hoped might someday qualify me for a full-blown assignment.

On one of my New York days I received an unexpected phone call from Myron Gollub, whom I hadn't heard from since he left for the naval training base in Pensacola. He was in New York and we arranged to meet for lunch. I expected him to have airborne tales that would rival Donohue's PT accounts and to be displaying a gaudy band of decorative ribbons on his Navy uniform, but when he came in the restaurant dressed in a civilian suit, his neck in a therapeutic collar, I knew he would not have a pretty story to tell. He had not only lost weight, but his wrestler's body was visibly diminished.

We ordered beers and, as always, Mo sighed deeply. "Here's to seeing you again," I toasted.

He sighed again.

"Were you shot down?"

"Nope. Neither shot up or down. Fact is, I never got my wings."

"How come?"

"I did okay at Pensacola. Got a good rating. Night before my group graduated, beautiful night, full moon like you only get in Florida, I wandered out to the airfield, decided to take a spin. There was a plane standing on the tarmac, so I climbed aboard, revved it up, taxied, got clearance, zoomed off. That plane normally requires a copilot, but I had flown it for heaps of hours and I knew I could handle it by myself. I cruised the starry skies an hour or so, then brought it home, clearing the tower, setting up for a landing like I made a million times before. Came down pretty and . . . crashed. Bad crash. Totaled the plane. Damn near totaled me."

"What happened?"

"Didn't perform the most important thing that a copilot does. The landing gear."

"Didn't lower it?"

"Right. Got washed out of the Navy. Just about washed *myself* out. But I'm coming back. A little at a time. How you doing?"

That's the way it had always been with Myron. Bright promise, dimmed by the unexpected. He was simply not programmed for success. After the war, he entered into a morose marriage, drank too much, and died too young, never having realized any of his potential.

I got along fine with my fellow staff members, who were friendly and helpful, especially Mark Murphy, who had written long profiles for *The New Yorker*. Mark was Irish through and through, as was his wife Mickey, also a writer. They lived with their two children in a house on a tree-lined street in the Park Slope section of Brooklyn and they sometimes invited me to dinner. Mark and I often had a drink after work before he took the subway home. He was a smiling, easygoing, ruddy-faced man who told wonderful stories about his exploits while researching articles. His most recent *New Yorker* profile was about a long-distance big-rig truck driver, a meticulous account of his haul from the East to the West Coast, an account that made the reader feel that he was sitting in the cab of the truck.

That Christmas Eve, Mark invited me to his house for dinner. The *Air Force* office closed early and Mark decided that he should buy a Christmas tree in Manhattan to take home to Brooklyn. First, however, we made a stop at Hurley's Saloon to inaugurate the Christmas season. As we left Hurley's we encountered a Christmas tree stand where Mark, feeling good from his Hurley's inaugural, selected a nice little spruce with full branches.

Now carrying his tree, Mark suggested a stop at P. J. Moriarty's, which was on the way to the subway station. P.J.'s had a festive Christmas group around the bar and Mark, one arm around his tree, his free hand around a glass of Bushmill's, joined lustily in a round of Irish songs caroled by the revelers. I tried to direct his attention to the time, but the group at the bar had now been considerably augmented by new celebrants and the volume of the selections, ranging from "Mrs. Murphy's Chowder" to "Deck the Halls," had become deafening, Mark's baritone making a significant contribution.

I finally managed to separate him from the Moriarty's imbibers, who had been trimming his tree with paper napkins, drink stirrers, beer coasters, and various fruits extracted from Tom Collinses and whiskey sours. Neither Mark nor the tree were looking so good—Mark had lost his khaki necktie and his overseas cap, rendering him out of uniform and subject to an unfortunate encounter with an MP patrol; in the process of its barroom decoration, the tree had lost some of its needles and a branch or two.

Mark held the battered tree against his body affectionately and, despite his unsteady gait, with my assistance we made it to the subway entrance, but he suddenly balked as we approached the steps.

"Hold it! Hold it!" he said. "I almost forgot Costello's. Gotta see ol' Tim. He'd never forgive me."

He stepped off the curb and flagged a passing cab. I tried to stop him, pulling at his treeless arm.

"Mark, wait a minute. Hold your flag, driver. Mark, it's nine o'clock. Mickey and the kids . . ."

"Just one drink. Never spent a Christmas Eve without having a drink with good ol' Tim. Gotta, gotta, gotta, just one, okay, one, promise."

He had the taxi door open. I tried to pull him back but there was no stopping him.

Costello's was even more packed and noisier than Moriarty's. Tim was indeed happy to see Mark, as were many of the Christmas revelers, who turned out to be friends of his from *The New Yorker.* This time the tree was placed on top of the bar and Tim trimmed it with beer-bottle caps, which he strung in strands and wrapped around the boughs. On the top he inverted a bottle of Guinness. I thought about calling Mickey but decided not to. I figured this scenario must have played many times before and I knew enough not to get involved in matters private between a man and a woman.

I made no further attempts to extricate Mark. The evening was lost and I figured Mark knew how to deal with wifely disapproval and crestfallen kids. It was eleven o'clock when we finally left Costello's. By now the tree was just a skeleton of what it had been, like a shuttlecock that had been battered in a fierce badminton match, and Mark looked no better. He was wearing the strand of bottle caps around his neck and a purloined tam-o'-shanter adorned his head.

I somehow managed to get him on the subway, where he promptly fell asleep, his head resting on what was left of his tree. I woke him at his stop, and after getting him through his front door, I returned to the subway for a sad ride back to Manhattan.

After the war, Mark returned to *The New Yorker* and we occasionally saw each other for lunch, his fondness for Bushmill's undiminished. I was more saddened than surprised when Mickey called me one day with the tragic news that Mark had died in a hospital in Nairobi, where he had been working on a piece for *The New Yorker*. He was forty-four years old.

# Eighteen

In the beginning of 1945, the war took a distinct turn for the better, and so did I. The army won the fierce Battle of the Bulge in the Ardennes Forest, and in the Pacific our forces landed on Bataan, Corregidor, Iwo Jima, and Okinawa. German forces were driven out of Northern Italy, and Mussolini was executed, his body hung by the feet in a public square in Milan. As for me, recently promoted to captain, I was given my first article assignment, the return of injured airmen to Westover Field and their rehabilitation, which resulted in this long-awaited directive:

ADDRESS REPLY TO
AIR FORCE EDITORIAL OFFICE
ONE PARK AVENUE
NEW YORK 16, N. Y.

TELEPHONE: MURRAY HILL 8-1981
TELETYPE: NY 1-2830

## WAR DEPARTMENT
## ARMY AIR FORCES

20 April 1945

SUBJECT: European Branch, AIR FORCE Editorial Office

TO : Captain Aaron E. Hotchner, 0563354

    Effective this date you are designated Chief, European Division, AIR FORCE Editorial Office, and placed in charge of such personnel as are assigned or will be assigned for duty in Europe. If directives from this office are not forthcoming, it will be your duty to determine the assignments of all personnel on duty from this office in Europe.

    By order of Lt. Col. Straubel:

HARRY S. RUSSELL
Lt. Col., Air Corps
Deputy Director
AIR FORCE Editorial Office

As head of operations, I would be able to give myself writing assignments for combat missions, and I intended to take full advantage of my autonomy. I applied for the earliest transport possible, and I was assigned passage on the *Queen Mary*, which, along with her sister luxury ship, the *Queen Elizabeth*, had been converted into a troopship in 1940. Painted camouflage gray, her ornate fittings and furnishings having been stripped and stored, the *Queen Mary* was equipped with armaments and refitted to carry five thousand troops. But after her first crossing, with the war going badly, the shortage of troops became critical, so by adding berths in stacks of six with only a foot and a half between them and with men sleeping in shifts and eating in shifts around the clock, her capacity was increased to a remarkable 15,740 troops and 943 staff for a total of 16,683, a capacity never equaled by any other troopship. She was able to deliver an entire division across the Atlantic in five days. A cabin-class stateroom designed for two passengers accommodated twenty-one men, sleeping eighteen inches apart. In the cabin-class swimming pool, berths were stacked seven high; thousands of men slept on the open deck.

The *Queen Mary* was, of course, a huge target for U-boats. It was estimated that there were over a thousand German submarines operating in the North Atlantic. From 1939 until 1945, when I came on board, 2,829 of our ships had been sunk by German torpedoes. In coastal waters, the *Queen Mary* was invariably escorted by two cruisers and six destroyers, but in the open Atlantic she was on her own, a sitting duck. But, incredibly, on her many crossings, the *Queen Mary* had never encountered a submarine, never was subjected to an air attack, and never had to fire her guns in defense of herself. This was primarily attributable to her speed, which exceeded twenty knots (34.5 mph), faster than the speed of enemy torpedoes. She was equipped with sonar detection and also followed an evasive zigzag course that consisted of frequent, unpredictable, alternating turns across its mean course of 106°.

My crossing was far below capacity. By now the bulk of our troops were already in the European theater, and the twelve hundred officers and four hundred WACs on board were mainly replacement personnel like myself. That first night at sea, I went out on deck and stood at the rail in the impenetrable darkness. Every inch of the teak rail that ran entirely around the ship had initials carved into it by the thousands of military men who had preceded me. It was a night without moon or stars, and as I watched the roiling water washing by, I thought of the hundreds of sunken ships and their crews buried on the bottom, victims of Nazi torpedoes. I wondered if any of those lethal German subs were possibly lurking in the depths beneath the black water, readying their torpedoes for an initial success against this noble ship.

I thought about what articles I would write as soon as I assigned myself to join the Eighth Air Force in England. I would accompany a particular bomber on a succession of combat runs, writing a series of articles about its personnel—the tail gunner, the bombardier, the pilot—trying to capture them at the time they were briefed at the airfield, in flight, during combat, and on the return to base. When writing about the bombardier, for example, I would try to make the reader feel that he was that bombardier approaching the munitions factory in Munich, readying his bombsight as the pilot held the bomber steady through a field of bursting flak, then opening the bay, and at precisely the right second releasing the bomb load for a direct hit, the munitions exploding in a mountainous roar as the pilot severely banked the bomber out of the repercussion area and away from avenging Messerschmitts.

As I walked down the deck, running my hand across the endlessly passing initials, I thought about how so many of those soldier-passengers who had carved those initials, going overseas for the first time, would never go back home, their initials on that teak railing their tombstones; I thought about the crews of our planes shot down over Germany, who perished with their planes in anonymous deaths, their bodies burned, the initials passing under my hand all that remained of them. I wondered if the Cunard people would preserve this teak graveyard.

# Nineteen

I spent each night of the crossing by myself in the prow of the ship, using the dark passage for cathartic meditation, feeling very close to myself. Strangely, I thought a lot about my father, trying to reconcile some of the antagonism I felt toward him. There were very few officers on deck, most of them in the bar below, and I was grateful for the distance of their conversation and laughter, as if they were in some faraway place and I was isolated in my own introspective orbit. That's when I confirmed my original hunch that I would not return to St. Louis and my career as a lawyer. If I survived the bombing missions I planned to go on, I would try to make my way in New York as a writer. Newspapers, magazines, advertising if necessary—any way I could find a foothold.

On the fourth night of our crossing, a day away from our destination in England, we were joined by the customary escort of two cruisers and six destroyers since coastal waters were the most likely to harbor U-boats. The night was brightened by a moon that occasionally surfaced between scudding clouds. I felt exhilarated by the silhouette of the gray flotilla of ships on each side of us. It made me realize that, aside from my few days in North Africa, for the first time I was actually in a war zone.

I became aware that the din of voices emanating from the bar had intensified perceptibly, actually becoming raucous roars as, without warning, all the lights of the *Queen Mary* blazed on in the night and virtually everyone on the ship came streaming onto the deck, shouting joyously, hugging, kissing, jigging around the deck. Across the water, the cruisers and destroyers also came ablaze with their lights, and a cacophony of their horns and whistles, capped by the thunder of the *Queen Mary*'s Klaxon, rattled the night. Then came the captain's ebullient announcement: "We have just received word from Allied Headquarters that the Germans have officially surrendered. A total cease-fire is in effect. The war is over."

A pandemoniac celebration broke out on deck, a bar quickly appeared, stocked with bottles from the *Queen Mary's* prewar reserve, and musical instruments, brought up from the hold, were commandeered by officers who had played professionally.

A pretty WAC lieutenant grabbed me and we whirled around to the music and drank from a passing champagne bottle until she disappeared, replaced by another and another as the makeshift band played lustily and arcing floodlights swept our faces. I was elated, and I was bewildered; there would be no more death and destruction, but I would never be in combat, never parachute from a disabled bomber, never help a crew escape through enemy lines.

The VE-Day party continued all through the night, right up to our docking in Southampton, where a vast crowd on the pier gave us a tumultuous welcome, as if we were conquering heroes.

I spent that year in Paris, running the *Air Force Magazine* bureau from its offices in the Hotel Scribe on the Boulevard Italienne. I dispatched articles for the magazine that dealt with aspects of the Air Force's role in the Army of Occupation, traveling into war-ravaged areas for my research. It was a period of fascinating transition, but I was dealing with the tragedy of aftermath rather than the struggle for victory.

I was separated from the service in 1946 with the rank of major, having spent four years in a quest for something that had eluded me. In the separation ceremony at Fort Dix, I was awarded four medals—American Campaign, European-African-Middle Eastern Campaign, World War II Victory, and Army of Occupation—

but I felt I didn't deserve any of them, not for a musical comedy, a movie, and some magazine articles.

All my life I have felt the imprint of those *Queen Mary* initials on my hand. My other strong memory is the spirit, the camaraderie, the sense of purpose and patriotism that pervaded this country during those war years, especially in the beginning, when things were going so badly. All of America seemed to be pulling oars in the same boat; possibly not since the Revolutionary War was the country so united, so dedicated, so driven toward a common goal. Sacrifice was commonplace. Honor was more than a Boy Scout oath. Pride was a motivation. Patriotism was our religion. Fraternity was a reality. A spirit that pervades the United States now, in the wake of September 11.

The war spawned the modern women's movement, opened our boundaries to the world, revolutionized our businesses and industries, furthered the cause of minorities, and improved tolerance, and to that extent I am grateful that I was in the States and able to witness these metamorphoses. The nation had become a family like never before.

That said, I'm still pissed about my lousy depth perception and my flat feet.